GARFIELD HIGH SCHOOL,
HOME OF THE BULLDOGS

Dick Selby

Copyright © 2012 Dick Selby
All rights reserved.

ISBN: 1475087497
ISBN 13: 9781475087499

DEDICATION

John Benson taught social studies, coached sports, and also worked as a dean at Garfield High School. He began there in 1965 and retired thirty-nine years later in 2004. In 1990, he was recognized as a "Teacher of the Year." Several of the teams he coached have won city championships, including volleyball, where his teams won two city championships, and softball. He has written two books about the techniques he has developed for teaching social studies: *Review Games*, and *Games Students Like to Play*.

John retired from Garfield in 2004, but his love for the students and his influence at Garfield was not to end. With a committee of dedicated alumni from Garfield, many of whom he taught or coached, together they have created the "John Benson Scholarships." These scholarships provide financial aid to graduating seniors. This year his scholarships will provide approximately forty thousand dollars in such aid.

Everyone benefits when teachers show dedication, compassion, and a willingness to go beyond the classroom to meet students' needs. It is because of the wonderful work that John Benson has done, over almost fifty years, that this book is dedicated to him. John, your presence, compassion, and willingness to help has been a guiding light for many thousands of students.

FOREWORD

There are many people to thank for this book: the teachers, the counselors, and the deans with whom I worked for so many years. I also need to thank the administrators. I know that without their ongoing support these psychological services that I was able to provide to the regular students would never have occurred. A special expression of gratitude goes to my wife, Barbara. She has endured the various difficulties that I experience at Garfield along with me, always providing her encouragement and her love.

In addition it is important to mention a guru from India, Sri Sathya Sai Baba. Sai Baba's spiritual influence, along with his philosophy of providing service to others, provided me with the emotional support that the kind of work I was doing at Garfield High School was exactly what I was supposed to be doing.

But mostly it is the students themselves who need to be thanked. During the many years I worked in the district, they were willing to open up their lives; permitting me to become a part of this challenging period of adolescence. It is because of them that I will forever be grateful and it is because of them that I have such wonderful stories to tell.

INTRODUCTION

My first job with the Los Angeles Unified School District was as a teacher at John Burroughs Junior High School. John Burrroughs was and continues to be one of the top intermediate schools in the city. After three years at John Burroughs Junior High School, I interviewed and was accepted for a counseling position at Lincoln High School in East Los Angeles. Though I did not have the necessary counseling credential, and it was not a requirement at that time, the principal, Pete Martinez, liked me and that was all that was necessary. Lincoln High School is located in East Los Angeles and the student body is comprised primarily of Latinos.

Then, after five years working as a grade counselor, I accepted a position that placed me in a variety of schools providing both individual and group counseling. It was during this two-year period that I completed my school psychology credential.

All but the first two student stories in this book pertain to Garfield High School and the work I did there as its school psychologist. I remained at Garfield for sixteen years.

Garfield High School became famous because of its math teacher, Jaime Escalante. Jaime taught calculus and challenged our inner city students to take the Advanced Placement Calculus Exam. A movie was made about Jaime's success. It is called "Stand and Deliver," and it came out in 1988. As a result of Jaime Escalante's successes, Garfield led the way for the kind of academic achievement that can be obtained within the inner city. Vice-President

George Bush, Sr., who later became president, visited the Garfield campus while he was campaigning for office in 1988.

Throughout the many years that I worked, I maintained a journal. It is this journal that has led to these stories. The names of the Garfield students have all been changed and in every story more than fifteen years have transpired since it took place.

Finally, it is possible that some of the specifics are not one hundred percent accurate. Even though I wrote down the important events as they happened, I acknowledge the possibility that some errors may have occurred. I also acknowledge the possibility that other people may remember these events and what happened somewhat differently than I. I believe, however, that each story presented here captures the difficulties and the importance of working with our children, as well as the kinds of situations that can be confronted as one works in the inner-city schools.

Enjoy now *Garfield High School, Home of the Bulldogs*.

CHAPTER 1

MY FIRST RIOT

The principal, Pete Martinez, liked me and he offered me a position as a grade counselor. I became the ninth grade counselor at Lincoln High School. It was 1973 and Lincoln's student population was more than ninety-five percent Latino. I will never forget the first day of class. The counselors were stationed in the school's auditorium where it was our job to program students who had something wrong with their schedule. Errors, I learned, were the norm.

Hundreds of students migrated in and out of this auditorium while we did the best we could to provide each of these students with classes. Tallies were maintained on a large bulletin board and, after programming the student, it was necessary go to this bulletin board and adjust the numbers. Most of the time these tallies were wrong, causing even more mistakes to occur.

First period ended and the passing period brought an influx of even more students. We now had the previous students to deal with, as well as the new ones who had just entered. *Wow,* I thought as I looked out to the auditorium, *we've got more students than ever.* I called up one student, made the tally adjustment on the bulletin board and sent her on her way. I called for another and as I did so I noticed a change in the noise level. For some reason it had become quiet, something not expected with so many students. I called out again and as I did so I watched a student go from one side of the auditorium to the other. This movement was all that it took and it was as though a canister of dynamite had gone off. The entire auditorium exploded. Boys fought boys, girls fought girls, and at times it seemed as though boys and girls were fighting each other. I later learned that the school's two major gangs had each come into the auditorium in force for that second period. It was my first day and we had a student riot. I could not help but wonder what I'd gotten myself in for when I accepted this job.

The counselors, school police, the deans, and any available teachers were called into the fray. Break up fights. Pull people apart and do whatever you could do to restore order. With all of us working together, the major troublemakers were rounded up and peace was restored, and through it all I was finding out what life was like on the East Side. I learned about gangs and that at Lincoln High School we had two major ones: Big Hazard and Clover. I also learned that we didn't have just two gangs, but within our school boundaries we had more than fifteen distinct gangs. And almost all of the students, whether or not they were official gang members, aligned themselves with one or the other of these major two gangs.

Later that first day, exhausted and with my mind reliving what had been an unbelievable beginning to my grade counseling career, I pulled my "VW" bug into the driveway. My wife had dinner waiting.

"We had a riot today," I began. "We were doing programming in the auditorium and then we had a riot."

"What do you mean?" There was a puzzled look upon her face.

"We had a riot. Everyone was fighting everyone else. Boys and girls fighting and it happened instantly. One second it was quiet and the next second 'boom.' It seemed like we had a hundred fights all at once."

Two terms I became familiar with were *cholo* and *chola*. *Cholo,* which is the term for a male gang member, frequently wore brown khaki pants, well ironed and heavily starched. A crease came down the middle of the pants' leg separating the two halves. This crease, and I never understood why this was the case, was cause for much esteem and served as a source of both *barrio* and gang pride. The occupant of these pants, as well as everyone else in the community, knew that this fastidiousness to one's dress immediately identified the person as a gang member, committed to the protection of his specific *barrio,* the neighborhood in which he lived. Some of the gangs we had were: Big Hazard, Clover, Lincoln Heights, Dog Town, Frog Town, Happy Valley, and Eighteenth Street. Long-sleeve flannel shirts were another part of the standard attire, usually falling loosely on the outside of the pants. Buttons were meticulously inserted in their proper places, from the bottom to the collar, with every button fastened. Shoes were characteristically of a heavy black-leather style and well polished.

Cholas, the female counterpart, had a somewhat larger and more expressive wardrobe. Like our male gang members, they sometimes wore the khaki pants with the well-pressed creases down the middle. This was not standard, but if they wore it, a belt would usually be pulled in tightly at the waist. The shirt was sometimes tucked underneath the belt, but it, too, could be worn outside and loosely fitting.

For the girls, hair spray was frequently applied. It might be used in such copious quantities that the hair seemed to sparkle in the daylight. Hairstyles varied, but a large mass of hair in the shape of a beehive was common. Eyebrows were frequently plucked, replaced with mascara, which formed a distinctive curve above the eyes. In a few cases, girls applied a white pancake make-up over the entire face. Then, with the mascara, white make-up, and a beehive above the head, a kind of Japanese Geisha image was presented. For anyone visiting the Lincoln High School campus for the first time, hearing more Spanish than English, and looking at the dress of some of these *chola* girls, it seemed as though Lincoln High School was not a part of the United States, but rather it belonged to some faraway and distant country.

Lincoln High School was my school for five years and I have memories that I will live with me forever. "Rosa and the Three *Cholas*" is one such memory.

CHAPTER 2

ROSA AND THE
CHOLAS

"**M**r. Selby," Rosa said as she moved forward. "Mr. Selby!"

I turned from my desk, putting away the last few papers, only to see the three of them: Rosa, Rose and Shelly, and they'd done it again. They'd caught me in my office. The bell had rung two minutes earlier and I was trying to finish, and now because of their visit I knew I'd be late to supervision. Rosa, the ringleader, came closer rubbing her index finger over her nose.

"How's your *nariz?*"

Nariz is Spanish for nose and I have a rather large one. This was an ongoing joke that played out frequently during their ninth grade year. Rosa was on the attack, closing in, and it was clear there was a sinister intent to her actions. She stepped closer while her two friends converged at the angles. I checked my escape routes and none were available. Then, when all three could see that I was cornered, Rosa took one step back and her friend Rose moved forward. Rose stood directly in front of the other two. Her long black hair came over her shoulders and half way down her back. Her complexion was light brown, almost olive in color, and a small, dark beauty spot on the left side of her cheek stood out.

"How are you feeling today, Mr. Selby?" she said coyly.

I didn't respond. Rosa and Shelly, however, stood close by and watched. Searching me out, confronting and teasing the rookie twenty-eight year old counselor, had become their pastime. Usually it didn't bother me, but today I was late. Rose came closer and closer while the other two stood guard. Closer and closer she came, and then, "Mr. Selby, how's your *nariz?*

"I have to go to supervision!"

They didn't move. I stood up from my chair and they locked arms blocking my path.

"Rosa, Rose and Shelly! You know I have to go to supervision."

Yes, they knew their game was coming to end.

"Let's go girls," as I pointed toward the door. "It's nutrition!"

Shelly, the third of this trio and the one who had been the quietest up to this point, decided the moment had arrived for her, too, to demonstrate her prowess. She moved in front of the other two and stared directly into my eyes, moving hers back and forth in a startling manner. They shook and vibrated in their orbits. Shelly smiled, satisfied with the end result, and the three of them burst into laughter. Their training of the rookie counselor was proceeding just as they had intended. Now they were now free to go to nutrition and discuss my progress and whatever else they could do to ensure my continuing education.

Rosa, Rose, and Shelly were all fourteen years old and they had formed a bond that would last throughout their high school years. They were innocent and having fun; but they also knew this was East L. A. Their high school and their homes were in the *barrio* and sooner or later the *barrio* has a way of coming back and striking you squarely in the face. It was about to be Rosa's turn and it would be an encounter that neither she nor I would ever forget.

The spring semester was just two weeks underway and it was a little after seven that Friday morning when I pulled into the high school parking lot. Five minutes later I sat at my desk beginning the process of organization and getting caught up with the required work. I continued diligently at my task when school started and then another bell rang. This second bell indicated that it was now homeroom. Students moved from their classes to a certain room to have the official role taken for the day, but I kept my door closed and locked. The head counselor had requested some specific information and I wanted to be able to provide him with it. I continued, focused to the best of my ability, but there appeared to be an abnormal amount of noise coming from just outside my exterior window. I stretched forward and looked, only to see that students were quickly gathering in this interior section. Lincoln High School was about to have another riot.

I sprang from my chair and rushed through the door, where I was swallowed up in a wave of students, bringing me through the large exterior doors to the outside.

"Fuck you," rang out.

The mass moved in the direction of the noise.

"Fuck you," came again, but from a different voice, and then... "You're dead. You're gonna wish you never done what you done. We're going to fuck you up good."

Battle lines formed as the members of the various gangs aligned themselves for what was sure to follow.

"Fuck you!"

An outside circle formed around the action; I pushed toward the center.

"Pegela, pegela!" (Hit her! Hit her!)

"Chingala, chingala" (Fuck her up! Fuck her up.)

I looked at the students who had gathered and my heart sank: Big Hazard, Clover, Dog Town, Frog Town, Lincoln Heights, Happy Valley, all of Garfield's toughest gangs, and who was in the center of the impending melee? It was Rosa; the Rosa who had been with her two ninth grade friends in my office just several days earlier. Rosa stood in the middle and with her were three of Lincoln's most difficult *cholas*. The *cholas* wore the characteristic gang attire of the day: khaki pants, pulled tightly in at the waist. Instead of a blouse they wore long-sleeved plaid shirts. Mascara and dark red lipstick were applied in abundance and when I looked closer I could see that one of the *cholas* had the characteristic white pancake makeup on her face.

My eyes moved from the four of them to the crowd. *Cholos* and *cholas* punctuated the surroundings, along with a large mass of on-lookers.

"Fuck you!" exploded from Raquel, the leader of the three. Then from one of the others came *"Cabrona"* (bitch) and the last one finished with *"Chinga tu madre."* (Fuck your mother.)

Rosa stood her ground, not backing away, but for Rosa escape was not possible. I checked for an administrator, someone recognized within the school with both position and authority, but there was none. Another counselor? Not a one. Not a teacher or one of our school police? Nothing! It was just me, the twenty-eight year old rookie counselor, while around me gathered the worst that this inner city school had to offer.

"The bell's rung," I screeched. "Let's go to class."

These words were accompanied with a determined look on my part, along with a motioning of my right hand. My fingers pointed in a direction away from this area and to some of the various homerooms where they were supposed to be.

"You're going to be tardy. Go to homeroom!"

"Fuck her up," came a voice from the crowd while not one of the students moved.

Realizing that what I'd been doing up to this point had served no purpose, I changed my strategy and stepped directly into the inner circle with the four of them.

"Let's go into my office. We can talk there."

They didn't move.

"Whatever the problem is, we can straighten it out in my office."

I couldn't help but wonder why I was alone. *Where were the other adults?* And I kept looking for assistance, but no one came and here's why. This impending riot had occurred at the worst possible of times. It was homeroom and teachers were where they were supposed to be, in their homerooms. It was Friday so the administrators were in their weekly meeting with the principal.

"Go to class! The bell's rung! You're tardy!"

Rosa moved to my side and distanced herself from the others. The leader of these three was Raquel and she reacted immediately: "You're dead." She pointed a finger angrily at Rosa, but Rosa and I had already begun this task of slowly moving away from the danger and to the school's central core.

"We can talk this over in my office," I stated and Rosa and I continued moving toward what we hoped would be safety. Raquel and the other two followed.

Raquel, however, was far from done: "You're gonna wish you never seen me. *Tu eres mia."* (You're mine.) Her face showed that she meant what she said.

Through the crowd, Rosa and I pushed. Threats and insults could be heard: "Let them fight. Let them fight." Sometimes the words were in English and at other times in Spanish, but for Rosa and me there would be no stopping. I kept a close watch on Raquel.

Because of my lunch and nutrition supervision I knew how difficult Raquel could be. She was part of Clover, which claimed the territory around the auditorium where I was assigned. No one, not even the boys, wanted to deal with her constant barrage of disparaging remarks. At one point I'd talked with the girl's assistant principal about her. I was informed that this assistant principal was doing what she could to work with Raquel and she believed she was making progress, though admittedly it was slow.

Raquel was about five feet, five inches tall and was one of the most attractive girls on Lincoln's campus. She used her looks, her anger, her intelligence, and her position of leadership to get whatever she wanted. She never backed away or backed down and when she was involved it meant trouble.

"I do the fighting," Raquel stated to her friends and to the crowd. "I do the fighting."

This was a fact that we already knew. When she was dressed in full fighting gear, sweatshirt and multiple rings on each finger, she was a fearless and dangerous opponent.

She again pointed at Rosa. "You've insulted my friend. You're nothing but dirt and I'm going to fuck you up. You're dead."

"I didn't do anything," Rosa responded, but her voice was muffled, faint.

Whatever had caused this confrontation and disagreement, and the threat of retaliation had to do with pride and the unwritten rules within the *barrio* and the gang. Rosa was being accused of something and would have to suffer the consequences. A process of retribution had been set in motion; the wheels of justice within the *barrio* move fast and with few constraints.

"I didn't do anything," Rosa stated again.

Rosa and I continued toward the exterior doors leading into the central building. Rosa, the three other girls and myself then entered the main corridor and arrived at the outside door to the counseling offices. Ten seconds later we were at my office; I pulled out my keys and opened the door. Rosa stood by my side and then entered while the others remained several feet to the rear.

"Let's go in," I stated.

The three *cholas* had come this far, but entering some sort of an enclosure was a risk they weren't sure they wanted to take. Was this a trap? If they entered, what might happen?

"We're here to talk. That's all. Let's talk."

Raquel entered and the other two followed. I closed the door. Paperwork was piled high on my desk. I pushed it to the side and then sat on the top of the desk. Rosa stood in the furthest corner to my left. The three others stood inside my door. At last we were ready to begin.

Silence.

I looked at Raquel and her friends, and turned to Rosa. What was I going to do? What was I going to say? And what was going on that had caused this sudden and unexpected outrage? I knew that we had experts within the school to handle these types of matters. One was Mr. Murphy, the boys' vice-principal, and we had Ms. Marchini, the girls' vice-principal. Both had more than twenty years experience working with gangs and gang related problems. We had the school police as well as our two deans. This role of handling gangsters and stopping a riot didn't fall into my job description, but on this day I would be going it alone.

"Okay, I began, "we're all here. The door is closed. It's just us. We can talk. What's happening?"

Not a word.

"We're here to talk."

It was quiet, and then...

"Slut!" Raquel was the first.

"*Puta,*" (slut) came from the girl on Raquel's left.

"Whore," came from the girl on Raquel's right. She was the one covered with white pancake makeup.

Rosa remained silent. She kept her head up and her eye contact was good. Though only fourteen years old, by her composure and ability to maintain eye contact she was demonstrating what I believed was an inborn toughness. She had what it takes to survive in this inner-city world of grudges, vendettas, and violence. What was happening to her was an integral part of the inner city and the *barrio*. And the reality was that any of these three gangsters could easily have handled Rosa, but it was to be Raquel, the toughest girl on campus and one of the recognized leaders of Clover who had insisted on this confrontation. It was Raquel, and this was because of her position with the gang, who had insisted on this challenge. Rosa stood quietly in her corner, keeping her head up.

These three threatened. They made gestures; they called her names, but Rosa showed no fear. She faced them straight on and looked directly in their eyes. I watched and knew I was witnessing the process of resolving issues in East Los Angeles gang style. I was the outsider, the rookie counselor who didn't speak Spanish, but for some reason on this day they had all decided that they trusted me. And they had all seen how I responded in our riots; we'd already had four of five of them. I wasn't afraid of confrontation, but I also didn't lose my temper and even in the heat of battle I was fair.

So what was it that had caused this powerful reaction? To them, Rosa had dared to become involved with a boy in their gang, and he already had a girlfriend, the girl with the white makeup. Rosa would have to suffer the consequences.

In this case the infraction wasn't quite the way these girls portrayed it. What had actually occurred was that the boyfriend had gone out of his way to walk Rosa to her early morning class. He was the one who had veered from his path and his standard procedure of accompanying his girlfriend. Rosa had expressed no interest in him and had even tried to separate herself, but he was the one who wouldn't leave. The boyfriend was the instigator, the guilty party. He was the violator of the rules, but to the three girls that fact was somehow irrelevant. By their rules the girlfriend had been wronged and because of this the entire gang had been offended. The girls of Clover had suffered emotional damage and Rosa, whether or not she was the responsible party, had to suffer the consequences. Rules, after all, are rules. That is the way society functions and that is the way a gang functions. There was a protocol that had to be played out if equilibrium, stability, and respect were again to be reestablished. And these three girls, with their actions and the discussion that followed, were part of the stabilizing process. They threatened. Rosa and I listened. They threatened some more and we listened some more.

Raquel's role as the respected leader had become a central aspect of this interaction. Gang leaders weren't automatically given this role, but they had to prove themselves worthy of the position. Once Raquel was informed of what had happened it became obvious. Some type of retaliation was mandated. Action was necessary.

So there we were. On one side was Raquel, the fighter and the leader of one of the most feared gangs in the East Los Angeles area and two of her closest companions. And on the other side was Rosa, fourteen years old, skinny, and with the backup of two goofy friends.

Progress was slow.

"Why were you talking with him?"

"I wasn't. He came up to me. I was walking to class. I don't even know him. He walked me to class."

"Why are you trying to steal him?"

"I'm not."

"Then why are you with him?"

Back and forth we went. Questions that had been asked were asked again and again. And where was that one administrator who could come to my aid? No one came. For me, on this day and at this time this was to be a solo performance, my one-man show. Were we making progress? I didn't know, but I knew it was important to continue the discussion and let them state whatever it was that they felt was necessary. If this were to be successfully resolved, the three girls from Clover were the ones in charge and any resolution was to be their decision and their decision alone. They would determine when and how to end this conflict. As this process continued I learned that there was a procedure to reaching that end.

Part one: Raquel needed to demonstrate that they had effectively punished Rosa, and it was unimportant whether or not Rosa was the instigator. Indiscretions like this happen all the time, and irrespective of whose fault it is, there are consequences. Rosa was a part of this community and she knew how it worked. She had to suffer.

Part two: Raquel and the other two girls needed to ensure themselves that Rosa was repentant.

"I won't talk with him," Rosa repeated. "I'm not going to try to steal him from you. He's your boyfriend. I won't talk with him. I'll stay away from him."

And when these two requirements had been met, Raquel had to be the one to take charge and decide that it was over.

"She can go," Raquel at last stated. The self-respect of the Clover girls had been maintained. Yes, Rosa could go free, and why not? After all, she was only a ninth grader and a goofy one at that. She wasn't like them. She didn't claim any backup of any specific gang.

It ended with a final declaration of peace and non-reprisal, and these three girls had done what their system dictated. They had restored their pride, and the respect of the girl with the boyfriend. And by following through with this ritualistic pattern this girl had validated her worth and her love for this *vato* (dude). For her it must have been true love. She was willing to fight for him, and what more could this *vato* ask from his *jeyna* (girlfriend)?

This was how it was done and an accord had been reached through hard knocks, intimidation and the constant risk of physical injury, but the tenuous equanimity of Lincoln's divergent gangs had been restored. Certain steps had to be taken and on this day there would be no riot and there would be no further repercussions.

The conference ended and I sent the three girls to their classes. Rosa remained for several minutes and we talked. When I was sure that she was okay, I sent her on her way. She had a smile on her face and I heard an excited giggle as she ran out the door. She had an amazing story to tell her friends. Then, as I leaned back on my chair, Mr. Murphy, one of the assistant principals, came to my door:

"Any problems here?"

"No. Everything is fine"

He turned and went back to the main office and his meeting, while I returned to my work. There was much to do. That's the way it was in 1974. I was young and learning my job, and this was to be an experience I would never forget. I remained at Lincoln High School for the next four years, but then it was time for me to change. I wanted to see what other opportunities were available in this large district. I transferred from Lincoln and worked as a counselor in a variety of schools and settings. At the same time that I did this, I obtained my school psychology credential. Little did I know I would be meeting both Rosa and her daughter twenty years later at Garfield High School, where I would be working as the school psychologist.

CHAPTER 3

A NEW CAREER

PART ONE

Having completed the requirements for the school psychology credential, I was at the onset of a new career. The district had been going through a financial crisis with cutbacks in just about every area, but school psychologists remained in demand.

It was in February of 1981 when I received my first assignment as a school psychologist: four elementary schools and one continuation high school and all of them located in the San Fernando Valley. I had never previously worked in what were considered to be white, middle class schools. I was about to find out what they were like.

I'm not sure which of the four elementary schools I visited first, but in the process of introducing myself, I traveled to each school. It was at one of these schools, and just as I was introducing myself to the clerical staff, that the principal rushed from his office.

"So you're the new psychologist," he said.

His shirt was tucked half in while the other half hung sloppily to the sides and to his back. A bulging mid-section protruded over a thick belt and an even thicker belt buckle. Several buttons on his short-sleeve shirt had loosened in the front, having pulled through their holes, while the others tugged tightly and stretched at their seams.

"I need to speak with you," he stated. Droplets of sweat formed into tiny balls upon his forehead and his western style tie moved slightly from the right to the left. He looked at me. "I have something very important to talk with you about."

Urgency was his style and, as the semester progressed, I learned that there was always a kind of "rush-rush" to his manner. And he was under the belief, like many principals within the schools, that he was the commander-in-chief. It was his school and his rules, and as its commander he needed to be informed of everything that was happening, no matter how insignificant or seemingly unimportant. The functioning of the school was processed through his constant need to micromanage.

He led me to his office where he sat behind a large desk and in a comfortable swivel chair. I sat in a standard wooden chair. He placed his hands behind his head and leaned back and looked me over. Once he had been informed that the previous school psychologist was leaving, he complained to my coordinator at the psychological services branch that he needed a psychologist at his school, a competent one, and as soon as possible. But now that he had me, what would I be like? Was I the school psychologist he desired? And the reality was that he wasn't looking for someone who was more competent than the last, but rather someone who would respond to his demands and who wouldn't challenge his authority.

After about fifteen seconds of giving me the once over, it was time for him to begin: "I spent twenty years in the navy. I was an officer, a commander. There's nothing like the military to teach self-discipline."

My head moved up and down, giving every indication that I agreed with him.

He leaned back in his chair: "You ever been in the service?"

"Yes, I spent six years in the National Guard."

The National Guard brought a surprised look on his face, but we both knew. People who joined the National Guard, and this was during the sixties, weren't interested in rendering real military service to their country. They weren't interested in learning the lessons that *esprit de corps* and following the chain of command had to teach. National Guardsmen weren't considered to be real soldiers. The truth was that they simply didn't have the training. (This, however, is no longer the case. National Guardsmen now make up a high proportion of the fighting forces.)

"Hum!" he responded. "I spent twenty years in the Navy."

I paid close attention.

"Went in right after college. Good training. Prepares a man for anything. See the world. Learn discipline."

He was watching and observing. Was I the psychologist that he desired? Would I do what I was told and follow his command? After about ten minutes, it was time to find out. He lowered his arms and pulled his chair snug to his large oak desk. Enough of this small talk, it was time for the commander to state his objective.

Leaning forward: "I want to talk with you about a student, a fourth grade girl who has not been attending her classes. All efforts have been made to get her back into school, but still she remains at home."

"What have you tried to get her back?"

"Everything, and nothing has been successful, either with the girl or with her mother, or with anyone else in the family. We've had many meetings and they still defy me."

I paid close attention to his use of the word "defy".

"It's been more than two semesters and she's not yet returned to school. The law is clear. It says that she has to be in school."

I could feel my heart pumping and adrenalin shooting through my veins. At last I was really going to be involved with a student. The many required college classes were the preparation, but now I was dealing with the real thing. And how difficult could it be to get a nine year-old fourth grader back in school? I'd worked in East Los Angeles with older students and I'd even been through at least ten riots. I'd dealt with some of the toughest gangs in the city. What could possibly be so hard about a fourth grade girl who doesn't want to come to school?

"This girl has to be in school."

"Yes, she does," I confirmed with a movement of my head.

A smile of satisfaction crossed his face. Yes, we were making progress.

"I'd like to speak with the teacher," I said and with that my first assignment was underway.

The girl's name was Olivia. I learned that she had been placed in the only special education class at the school. She was classified as learning disabled, which meant that her overall ability was within an average range, but her academic testing in reading, writing and mathematics was below grade level. And though this girl had never attended our special education class, the teacher had been involved in several meetings with the mother and the grandparents. This teacher would have important information to provide and I needed to talk with her. Feeling a rush of enthusiasm, as well as being emotionally ready to demonstrate my expertise as a school psychologist, I would begin work on this case immediately.

I arrived at the special education class just as the bell rang for recess. I opened the door as twelve students sat in four straight rows; their hands were crossed and placed firmly on the tops of their desks. The teacher stood at the head of the class with her arms staunchly folded in front of her, presenting a firm and authoritative manner. She watched each student closely. If these students wanted recess, they had better control their behavior. The air was still as she stood motionless and you could hear a pin drop. When at last she was sure that her behavioral requirements had been satisfied, she began the process of calling each student by name. This student then walked slowly to the exterior door and, without any display of exuberance, quietly stepped outside.

Two minutes later, and after the last student was released, I introduced myself. Immediately I became aware that she was well informed and quite knowledgeable about the problematical situation. She also had strong opinions about how this girl should be handled.

"Mother is to be held accountable," she began, "but grandfather is the real 'sicko.' Grandfather is causing all of the problems. He's crazy and he's a sexist pig. Grandfather is a total tyrant and this child is emotionally sick. Olivia is a poor nine-year old who is extremely introverted. In fact her introversion is so bad that she does not fit into a regular public school or into this special education classroom. Her needs are just too great. She should be placed into a non-public school and as soon as possible. Olivia needs to be placed in this protected environment because she is seriously emotionally disturbed and she needs constant supervision."

An easy case? I was getting an entirely different perspective about this case and my presumed easy solution. School phobias and poor school attendance can be challenging and time consuming, but severe emotional disturbances and non-public school recommendations require the greatest of professional expertise. Olivia, this fourth grade student, was to be my first case. I'd originally wanted to work into this new job and its requirements slowly, in order to build up my expertise and my confidence. Was I ready to handle such a difficult case?

"This girl should not be in a public school," she emphasized. "She is so emotionally sick that she needs to be placed in a non-public school."

The bell rang and noise could be heard from the outside. Several boys were pushing each other back and forth and a girl started to cry. A stern look came across the teacher's face. It was time to return to being teacher and authoritarian. I thanked her and quietly walked out.

After this discussion, I was feeling uneasy about the recommendations of the special education teacher. I decided it was best for me to talk this case over with my immediate supervisor and give him some of the most recent information. After all, he was classified as a senior psychologist and had worked as a school psychologist for more than twenty years. He had the experience, the authority, and the wisdom to guide me during this evaluation process and to properly supervise me as I completed my initial case.

This was what he said: "She starts school there and soon or she'll have to go to Kingston. The previous psychologist told me that this student is psychotic. And if they don't like that, (referring to the mother and the grandparents) we'll contact DCFS (Department of Children's and Family Services). We can have her removed from the home for not going to school."

He added that he was sick of the problems that this girl and her mother, and the grandparents had created, and that this girl was nothing but a troublemaker. Olivia and the problems related to her were the primary reasons why the previous school psychologist had accepted a position in another school district.

My initial exuberance had taken a turn for the worst, but I didn't lose heart. There was one last person to contact and that was the previous school psychologist. She had participated in several of the conferences with the parent and the grandparents and maybe she could provide some additional and, hopefully, more positive information? After all, in the scheme of things, when I would write this case up, she was the expert and her opinions would carry the most weight. I called to the school where she was now employed.

"This girl has a very severe school phobia," she began, "and she is psychotic on top of that. I also believe, though I can't prove it, that the grandfather has sexually abused her. He's a misogynist who dominates all the women in his life and he preys unmercifully upon this poor young girl. Because of this grandfather believes, and he is an ex-drill sergeant from the Marine Corps, that by his will he can do whatever he wants. This girl will never be normal and everyone is afraid of him. It is because of grandfather, a sex fiend, that she has no chance."

No suspected abuse case had been filed. This was also before the Los Angeles Unified School District took precautions to ensure that whenever suspected abuse was considered, it was mandatory to file a report with the Department of Social Services.

"I can't prove it," she continued, "but this guy is a real sicko."

Three strikes and you are out... that is all you get in baseball. This was my third strike. Was there any hope for this nine year old who seemed to meet all of the qualifications for the most severe academic placement imaginable, placement in a non-public school?

Psychosis, sexual abuse, introversion, school phobic, all of these appeared to play a significant role and I hadn't even met the girl yet. I was beginning to wonder if I had made a good decision by going into school psychology in the first place. I was also going to be dealing with a family that had all the appearances of being extremely dysfunctional. What other psychological abnormalities and diagnostic findings might turn up as I completed what was to be my first psychological evaluation?

CHAPTER 4

A NEW CAREER

PART TWO

I phoned Olivia's mother and arranged for a meeting. The two of us would be able to discuss the previous attempts in getting Olivia back to school as well as her adjustment at the present time. I explained that it would be necessary for me to do a basic psychological evaluation and that this testing would last no more than thirty minutes. Within this short time period, it was my task to determine if Olivia, who had not attended school for more than a year, could be successful in our elementary school environment.

I did not tell mother of the recommendations from these others and that my evaluation was perfunctory in nature, but I knew the truth. I, as a rookie school psychologist, was simply satisfying the basic criteria that my supervisor indicated was necessary. Because

I was the one officially authorized to be in charge of the meeting, it was a requirement for me to meet with this girl and with her mother. And, if it were possible, I should complete a basic evaluation. The decision about eligibility and placement, for all practical purposes, had been made. Olivia would be sent to a school for the seriously emotionally disturbed. In this restricted environment the school's specialists would help her and her mother to understand that she was very sick and that Olivia needed special treatments and medications. They would classify her emotional illness in a way that would help others to more fully understand the seriousness of her problems. I knew that with certain students special schools could be very beneficial. And in this case it was my duty, my obligation, not only as a professional but also as an inexperienced school psychologist, to listen to the wisdom from all of the others and do as I was told: follow the chain of command and do what my immediate supervisor was recommending. Non-public school, according to all of them, was the only option. But as I proceeded my thought was: *is this really the correct placement?*

Three days later I sat in the nurse's office where I would conduct my evaluation. I looked at my watch and it was two-thirty; they should arrive at any minute. I noted the austere interior of this room. Nurse's offices are typically decorated with pictures, drawings by students from all of the different grade levels, stuffed animals and children's games, but in this office there were only barren walls. Several metal folding chairs were placed next to one of the walls and that was all. The absence of any outward sign of life, or of children and compassion, was the obvious indication of our troubled educational times. The cutbacks had been dramatic. Not only had there been increases in class size and fewer counselors, but also school nurses had been reduced to a bare minimum. The nurse at this school was there only one day a month and her primary task was to complete paper work. Rarely was she directly involved with the students or with anyone else.

A small window facing to the outside was located above the metal folding chairs and I moved toward it. As I stretched my body high to get a good look, I saw two people approaching. It was Olivia and her mother, and they simultaneously adjusted their gait as they marched up our central walkway. Mother thrust each leg forward in a militarized cadence, while Olivia clenched to the upper section of mommy's left thigh. Their forward motion was jagged and serpentine, moving first in one direction and then the other. I estimated mother's age to be in the late twenties or early thirties; she was slightly overweight. Her hair was of medium length and with no particular styling. As I watched them approaching mother gave the outward impression of being stressed to the max and of having reached the limits of her ability to adjust. They entered the main office and I heard, "We're here to see Mr. Selby."

The secretaries sent them in my direction and within seconds came a gentle knock and a muffled, "May we come in?"

I walked to the door. Mom wore a plain blue and white dress, and clinging to her leg and tugging on her dress was Olivia. I reached forward to shake mother's hand and then crouched low to Olivia.

"Nice to meet you."

Olivia pulled her head from one side of mother's leg to the other, with an obvious showing of discomfort and fear. As I watched her behavior, I realized that I should not place any type of emotional pressure upon her. I knew that in dealing with Olivia I would have to be very careful. I pulled away and straightened my body. I turned my attention to mother, while Olivia remained half hidden, pulling the folds of mother's skirt over most of her body. Two eyes peeked out.

"Here are some chairs," I said, indicating that we should all sit down. Mom moved to one of the chairs and sat, but as she did so Olivia found herself being squashed between the metal chair and mom's upper thigh. Then, deciding that this wasn't the position she had hoped for, Olivia squeezed toward the front where she plopped herself down on top of mother's foot.

I observed and took note of everything that was happening. This was important information that would aid in the writing of my first psychological evaluation. I watched Olivia with her movements that were shaky... and her body reacted with each word that I spoke. Finally, when she could see that I had made no externally threatening moves, she stuck her thumb in her mouth and squeezed herself as far away as she could, sticking her head safely behind mother's leg.

It was time to begin: "I'm glad you're here." My voice was soft, but with each word I heard squeaking sounds. I lowered my voice even more, but still she squeaked. I tried not to notice as her body shook and convulsed. I tried not to react to the various expressions of fear that were directed at me, or to her cheeks as they moved in and out with each inhalation and exhalation upon her thumb. I slowed my enunciations and patterned myself after Mr. Rogers from "Mr. Rogers' Neighborhood." This seemed to help as two eyes peered at me from deep behind mother's leg.

I explained the purpose of the interview and of the evaluation. This was a simple process and one that was required if I was to have a basic understanding of Olivia's functioning. I knew that her behavior during this evaluation process would be a most important part of my final case write-up. I explained that I was only concerned with the most basic of information: reading, writing and arithmetic skills, and there was one drawing test that I would also administer. With this test, it was necessary for Olivia to copy nine shapes from some cards. It provides important information on both basic reading capabilities and emotional functioning. Olivia watched attentively from a safe distance and listened to my every word. Her external noises had decreased, but I was not yet ready to begin.

I went to my arsenal of school psychology "helpful essentials and handy-dandy odds-and-ends" that were to be employed in times of an emergency: toys, puppets, and other types of play things that were jam-packed in an old attaché case. With this variety of toys, taken from my own children's toy collections, I found myself in the process of completing my first official assessment. So, with Olivia still looking on from behind mother's leg, I pulled out one of the puppets, placed it on my hand and began talking through it. This inanimate figure transformed into a vibrant and extrovert personality.

Olivia's face lit up, but this was not a process that could be rushed; she wasn't going to be easily convinced to participate in this testing or to let her guard down. If I were to be successful, I would have to do more than just pull some cute puppet out of an old briefcase. I would have to create an atmosphere where Olivia's standard emotional reactions could somehow be eliminated. And in order to do this I would have to use every skill that I had and every insight to pull her into a world where she would feel comfortable enough to let go of mother's leg and join me on the floor for the testing.

And I knew: if she were unable to leave mom, or if I stopped this testing procedure at any point before completion, her inability would be the surest indicator of her emotional sickness and inability to adjust. She would be classified as severely emotionally disturbed and would be going to a school for those with the severest of emotional problems. But "hope springs eternal" and maybe, just maybe, I might be able to accomplish what the others had not.

I held my puppet high and it was time to take the first big step. This was my favorite puppet and it was of a little girl with long blond hair, a blue dress, big eyes, and large, blond eyelashes. The puppet came alive: "Hi! I'm Sandy. Do you like my hair?"

Sandy turned one hundred and eighty degrees, showing off her long blond tresses. While this was happening I moved from my chair to the floor. I held the puppet in front of Olivia, who continued to be hunched behind mother's leg; my actions were designed to integrate with Olivia's responses. I remained at a safe distance. Olivia made a few initial screeches but her eyes remained focused upon her new-found friend.

Sandy continued: "Do you like to play? I like to play. Later you can play with me." Sandy turned and searched the briefcase, a *potpourri* of only the most exciting of toys and announced: "There are more toys in here. You can play with all of them."

Sandy picked up several of the toys with her mouth, flopped them up and down and dumped them back inside the briefcase. Then, with head facing directly to Olivia and with her mouth open, Sandy moved up and down in a positive, encouraging fashion.

I put the puppet down and spoke to Olivia about what it was that I needed to have her do. I showed her the four tests and explained again that none of them would take long. Mother would be right here with us the entire time. Sandy again jumped into action giving the appearance of excitement and enthusiasm.

"What do you think?" Sandy asked. "Let's give it a try?"

Sandy was placed on the floor adjacent to the test area. The moment we had been waiting for had almost arrived. I looked at mother, again assuring them that we would all stay in the office. And I repeated to Olivia that if she desired she could stay and play with the toys after we were finished with the testing. One more puppet came into action and it was none other than Superman, the man of steel, and out of the briefcase he flew. Soaring and sailing he did a loop-de-loop and crashed into the waste paper basket. But this man of steel was unperturbed by his encounter with some sort of recycling canister. He brushed himself off and resumed his flight pattern, only this time flying close to Olivia.

"So what do you think lassie?" he asked. Superman beckoned to her as he soared by and his cape waved up and down. This man of steel, of red and blue, surprisingly had a Scottish accent. "Are you ready?"

We were about to find out. Olivia looked at him and her eyes grew large. A smile crossed her face as he did a few more loop-de-loops and came to a screeching halt. Mother did not move but her eyes watched the various activities. Superman's head moved joyously up and down, indicating that the time had come. He then performed a perfect landing adjacent to the brief case and lay down.

Everything was positioned where it needed to be in the center of the floor. The testing materials were in open view and did not appear to be overly threatening, and without prompting or encouragement, Olivia moved towards the center of the floor and the materials. Mother quietly positioned herself several feet away.

These tests were minimal and my expectations were even less than that, but in over a year no one had been successful in getting even this far. I began with the drawing test of the nine different forms and then proceeded to the reading, writing and math. Throughout, Olivia maintained a desperate, pleading manner and consistently looked in the direction of mother, but she did not stop taking these tests, and perhaps just as significant as Olivia's reaction was mother's. Mom did not give in to these pleas and outward projections of fear. The terrified expressions, the shaking and the fear, which were so prevalent when they entered the nurse's office twenty minutes earlier, were reduced. Screeches came sporadically, but my approach was not to show any reaction to them. I acted as though I had not heard anything. Olivia and I sat on the floor working and the minutes ticked by, one by one, but in this office the three of us were pulling together and something was happening.

When the testing was completed there was a feeling of accomplishment by all of us. I put the test materials down and Olivia decided that she wanted to play. She was especially fascinated with Sandy, our out-spoken female puppet and advocate of female equality.

This interlude provided me with the opportunity to talk with mother. She explained that both she and the grandparents wanted Olivia back in a regular school. Yes, they realized this little girl of theirs had learning problems and needed special help but they didn't want her in a special school. Other people, and at this point she was referring to the previous school psychologist, the special education teacher, the principal, as well as a variety of well-intentioned others, had threatened them with a non-public school and even legal retaliation. A non-public school was not what any of them wanted and they felt such a placement was inappropriate. Olivia continued playing.

"Let's see what we can do," I responded.

My apparent optimistic appraisal of the situation somewhat surprised me, but we had gotten this far and maybe there really was hope? Maybe all of the previous experts had been wrong? *Most certainly,* I thought, *experts have been wrong in the past in regard to other cases, and perhaps they are wrong now.*

I told mother that the regular school placement needed to be given a try. Mother nodded in agreement while Olivia dumped all of the toys from the briefcase onto the floor. As preparation for this re-entry, another meeting was arranged and the grandparents were also to be involved. I knew that if we were to be successful we would need to have the full cooperation of everyone, including grandfather.

This second conference was scheduled in two days at nine in the morning. Several minutes prior to this meeting, I sat in the same chair and reviewed the test results. I looked over Olivia's drawing test, the Bender. To the untrained eye it appeared to be innocuous, but for someone familiar with the variations of the patterns it provided a wealth of information. I analyzed the strange ways Olivia had drawn three of the forms and these responses were indeed indicative of some emotional adjustment difficulties. But were these emotional indicators so strong and debilitating as to prevent her from attending a regular public school? I couldn't answer this and neither could anyone else. The only way to make this determination would be to put her into the classroom and see what would happen. Tests, after all, are only tests.

I reviewed the academic results (reading, writing, and arithmetic) and her scores were reflective of someone who needed additional help, but that was why she had been placed in the special education program in the first place. My eyes scanned the nurse's office. It seemed even more barren than during my previous conference. Four empty walls without a hint of life. What was going on with education? My eyes again focused on the office's one window and I went over and raised high to take a look. My interviewees were on their way.

Grandfather was the leader. He walked rapidly and by his outward demeanor it was clear...here was a man with a purpose. I wasn't sure what this purpose was or what his intentions might be, but I knew I would be soon be finding out. Grandmother was next and she struggled with each step to maintain the rapid pace of her partner. Finally came mother. She followed several steps behind the other two, and like grandmother she was having difficulties maintaining the pace.

I returned to my cushioned chair behind the desk, took several deep breaths and waited. Grandfather was the first to enter the central office and without hesitating or saying anything to the secretaries he came directly to my office. He knew what he was doing and where he was going. He stood at the door, which was partially opened.

"Well, I'm here," he stated, and not waiting for a response he entered. His hair was short, in crew-cut fashion. He wore a tight white T-shirt and a spattering of gray chest hair reached over the top, curling tightly upwards and towards his neck. A large tattoo representing the Marine Corps was visible on his well-muscled arms. He was six feet tall, two hundred pounds and in his early fifties.

I rose from the nurse's chair and came forward to greet him: "I'm Mr. Selby." I reached to shake his hand but he immediately turned away. He was not happy about what had happened during the past year and this was his way of demonstrating his continuing displeasure. For him, there were to be no smiles, just business. He had seen it all, done it all, and as a drill sergeant he had been trained to break down the best of them. No matter what situation he found himself in, he was in charge.

Grandmother entered next. While grandfather projected hostility, she was timid and fearful. Several seconds later mother pushed through the door and entered, huffing and puffing. She found herself a chair. Just as the previous experts had warned, grandfather ruled. The two women sat close together while grandfather remained standing, maintaining a steady and cold stare. I sat down and did not return his stare.

I began: "We need to see if we can get Olivia back in school."

We were underway. Grandfather, and with no hesitation: "You're the ones who caused all of the problems. You're the ones that changed her school and changed her teacher. She was doing just fine. She liked the other class and she liked the other teacher. She don't like this teacher!"

Grandfather was referring to the fact that prior to being assigned to this school, Olivia had been attending another school approximately two miles away, but that special class had been closed. There weren't enough students, so the few students that there were sent to different schools throughout the district. Grandfather stated his complaint about the other class being closed and I listened. This was the first that I had heard of this school change, but I also knew that the opening and closing of special education classes throughout the district was common. Rather then discussing issues over which I had no control, I decided it was best to concern ourselves with the current problem.

"There is nothing we can do about this classroom and school change. But now we need to get her in school."

Time has a way of changing priorities and the manner in which we view things. Grandfather's anger previously had served a purpose. He was angry about the change of schools and this new teacher that none of them liked. But Olivia had not been in school for more than one year. Not only was she missing out on her education and the important socialization that she needed, but also at home she was unhappy and making a poor adjustment. Each day she required much of their time and she was becoming even more demanding. After more than a year, everyone at home now fully recognized that she needed to be in school.

Mom leaned forward: "We have to do it now. We can't let her crying stop us any more. Daddy, she has to be in school." We looked at each other. It had taken almost a year and half to reach this conclusion and now it was so obvious.

A strategy was devised that would begin the following day, based on scientifically proven psychological techniques called behavior modification. Behavior modification, the watchword of the day, consists of a variety of well-outlined behavioral modification procedures. For the behavior modification specialist, behaviors and their concomitant emotions are seen as a result of certain reinforcements and for the behavior specialist (the university professor at UCLA or Stanford) the procedure is to modify or change the environment and the reinforcers so that the appropriate behaviors and emotional reactions are obtained. With these behavior specialists, it all comes down to analysis and the development of a behavior intervention strategy.

We agreed on the strategy and, if I had done my homework properly and, if my college professors had been right, things would proceed smoothly. Just stick to the recipe and that is all.

In final preparation for the next day's procedures, I discussed the plan with the teacher: "You're wasting your time," she said. And not only that, she was visibly upset that I had not just automatically held the meeting that would place this girl in a non-public school. She turned and walked away. She was clearly unhappy about the intended intervention. Ten seconds later, "There is no way that this girl will fit into the classroom."

What works with a college professor in convincing people to try a system of behavior modification doesn't necessary work with someone who does not have the same professional credentials. The teacher was angry, but I had done my part and informed her of the attempt that would be made. After talking with the teacher, I went to talk with the principal. He sat behind his desk and kept staring at me. I explained the plan, but from his expression he was equally as unhappy about this attempt as was the teacher. Why would I be trying something such as this when the school simply wanted to get rid of this troublemaker and her grandfather? This was clearly not what the principal had in mind when I began this process. I could see that he was questioning himself as to whether or not I was the right psychologist for this school. Finally, and it did take him some time: "Just get her in school," and he turned away. I realized I was on my own with this behavior modification strategy and decided not to call my immediate supervisor. But on the other hand I believed that there was something positive that was happening.

As I walked to my car at the end of the day I questioned myself about what I was attempting. *What if this plan doesn't work? What if these behavioral strategies that these university professors taught with so much pedagogical expertise are ineffective?*

I was not in the college classroom and I was no longer a student. I wasn't dealing with something that was theoretical or that would be done under the university's highly controlled testing conditions. My professors would not be available for me to ask questions. With a mind filled with doubt, I got in my car and headed home. Tomorrow the proof of my undergraduate and graduate studies would be shown to those who counted most: Olivia, mother, grandparents and, of course, the special education teacher and the principal. What had I gotten myself in for?

CHAPTER 5

A NEW CAREER

PART THREE

I arrived at seven-fifteen the following morning. Though class did not officially begin until eight, there were some last minute preparations to be done. The classroom teacher and I were supposed to begin the adjustment process by meeting with the mother and Olivia at seven-thirty.

When I entered the office I was given the bad news: both the principal and the teacher had called in sick. *This is really strange*, I thought. *Neither seemed very happy about my plan to bring Olivia back into school.*

But I knew that with or without them I would be following through with the modification strategy. The secretary informed me that a substitute teacher had been assigned and that she was already preparing her lessons for the day. I went to the classroom and knocked. She opened the door and we introduced ourselves. She was approximately forty years old and, after explaining the intended strategy, I felt good about having her in the classroom.

I now only needed Olivia and mother, but at seven-thirty they were no shows. It was five minutes later when mother arrived, panting heavily and somewhat out of sorts. She was alone.

"Olivia refuses to obey me." Mother was very upset about Olivia's behavior. "She came with me to the school, but she refused to come to the room. She's standing in the parking lot beside the car."

I looked at mother. I had previously thought that we might have a few unexpected difficulties, some glitches along the way, but we hadn't even started. The acclimation process in the behavioral modification strategy was considered to be a most important aspect in getting her back to school, but how were we going to do this now? I considered taking the easy way out, to simply give up and do what all of the professionals already wanted and put her in a non-public school. I looked at mother. She was very upset and had lost control of her daughter. Was it time to throw in the towel and call it quits?

"Let's go." I said.

I knew that the only way to have an answer to our question was to actually put this girl in the classroom. Mom and I proceeded to the parking lot. I had made a commitment and I was going to see it to the end, whatever that end might be. We came around the last corner in the main building and off in the distance we could see Olivia, standing next to the car and watching. We had not taken more than two steps when Olivia took off in the opposite direction. Mom and I watched as our nine year-old, wearing long pink pants with pink tennis shoes, and with pigtails flailing from one direction to the other, charged down the block and turned the corner, and wow, that skinny girl could run.

Mother shrugged her shoulders. "It's hopeless," she moaned.

Was there nothing more that could be done? However, that morning I had decided to wear my Adidas running shoes, just in case the unexpected might happen, and now I had a runaway fourth grade girl on my hands. With mother standing there, I took off in my sprint mode after the psychotic, sexually abused, emotionally disturbed, pigtails flailing, not to be captured nine-year old. Down the block and around the corner I charged... and here we were: Olivia, seventy pounds, and me, two hundred and ten. Big, burly man chasing skinny kid. What did the neighbors think? It was too late to ask. Did my professors ever chase their clients? I doubted it. Was I doing the professional thing? Good question, but my adrenalin had kicked in and my client was a runaway.

I watched her run past two families deep in conversation standing on their front lawn. Olivia dashed by and not one head or eye strayed from their stationary positions. About fifteen second later I, too, came running by. I smiled, but just as with Olivia, no one looked. No one noticed. Then, with head down and arms churning, I barreled on.

When I had gone about a block and a half from the school I could see in the distance that she had stopped. She stood in one spot momentarily trying to gather herself for a second effort, but before she could again resume flight I arrived. I placed my hand on her shoulder, turned her around and we began the journey back. Time I knew was of the essence and though the first part of the plan did not in any way resemble our intended format, there were other parts of our strategy still needing to be utilized. *Hopefully,* I thought, *I can get her into the class before the other students arrive.*

Unfortunately, we were still more than two full blocks from school. She then took only five or six mini-steps and came to a standstill. She sat on the ground, pouted, tensed her body, and she had made up her mind. She wasn't going to be put in anyone's classroom, not on this day, not tomorrow, not ever.

I towered high above her and it had come down to a contest of wills and who was going to win? Big burly man or skinny nine year-old? I looked down and she was digging her heels into the ground. I looked around for help, but there was none. *How had I gotten myself into this mess in the first place?* I looked down and she looked up. *My psychology professors never indicated that this type of unexpected event could happen.*

Finally, reality sank in. It was just the two of us and there was no assistance coming my way. I reached down and she grabbed her ankles and tensed her body. Her head turned upward and fire sprang from in her eyes. "Oh what the heck," I blurted out and I picked her up. I then carried her for those two blocks back to the school.

Now, just as we approached the school, I noticed a group of older boys congregated on the opposite side of the fence. These were sixth grade boys who had witnessed the sequence of events. They saw her running away and me chasing after her and they saw me bringing her back. While I walked toward the school's entrance, they yelled, "Let her go! Let her go!" I walked on, but it was also at this exact point that I learned an important lesson in life, and this was what I learned: You are not going to get away with anything from sixth grade boys. Forget it! They're too tough. They called me names and started throwing rocks. One rock hit me. Six adults stood in their front yard talking as both Olivia and I ran by and they didn't notice. They didn't notice when I carried her back. And now just as I was nearing my final destination, these sixth grade boys attacked.

At last the bell rang and the boys went to their classes; I could continue. Olivia's mother was directly ahead and standing by her car. Part of the plan had called for mother to be with Olivia during the earliest transition into the classroom, but it was too late for the transition phase. A slight change of plans was necessary. Olivia and I approached the parking lot and I motioned to mother to get into her car and go home. "I'll handle it from here," I stated. "I'll call you later."

As I watched mom drive away I could feel myself preparing for the next phase. I picked up this nine year-old and carried her the remaining distance to her class, but her manner had now changed. Instead of being quiet and compliant, she kicked and made screeching noises. I responded several times with, "We're going to your class." I squeezed her tightly so that she couldn't escape.

In about two minutes, we arrived. The outer door was closed and I let her down. She stood quite still and simply stared, and she did this in a calm manner. She brushed off her pants. It was during this interlude that I noticed the surrounding quiet of the school. Everything was serene and peaceful. Students were in their classes learning, but something significant was happening in this faraway corner: before the two of us was one last obstacle, the closed door. Should we go in, or should we back away? She looked at me with a stony stare and her eyes glistened. She again brushed off her pants, but I could see. She was preparing herself. Who did I think I was?

Destiny had brought us together and we both knew that once we went through this door we had an audience that was ready, willing and waiting. And what about the strategy, those scientifically proven techniques? They had disappeared with the rock to the head. It was now just Olivia and myself and it was winner take all. I reached for the door while Olivia and I looked at each other one last time. We were at round fifteen. She gave a quick swat on her pants. The time had come.

I opened the door and we entered. All eyes were upon us: the substitute teacher, the aide, and the twelve students. We inched our way forward while I searched out what was the one empty chair. There it was: one empty chair had been placed between two of the girls and Olivia innocently and obligingly took her place. She sat down and her arms flopped on the top of the desk. I backed away. She was as quiet and still as a church mouse, and then, "bang," like an explosion she burst into action. Up and out of her seat she flew, towards the far door, and not only was she fast, but she had the moves of an NFL star. Darting here and dashing there, she slashed through the other children, and I dashed after her. She reached the door and was half way out, but I caught her before she could cross the goal line. Squirming and kicking, I brought her back to her seat, arms and legs flailing, head and body churning in every direction. I squished her down.

"Olivia is just getting adjusted to the school," I announced. All eyes were upon us. "She'll be fine when she gets to know us," and I continued squishing.

Olivia was jammed into her desk and as I released and stepped back, she wasn't done. Up, out, around, and through the class she ran. Three times, four times, five times, again and again. She was quick and elusive. Underneath the desk, out the side of her desk, through the center of the students, around the students, and a few times she went between their legs, but the end result was the same. I caught her each time.

"She'll be fine," was my response, but she didn't look fine. She squirmed, kicked, thrust and wiggled, but I brought her back and squished. "She's just getting adjusted."

Olivia didn't look like she was getting adjusted, but after about half-an-hour of this escape routine something was happening. She slowed in her attempts and the temporary periods of inactivity were gradually increasing in length. Perhaps it was exhaustion, though I don't think that was it. I think she was getting adjusted in a strange sort of a way to the class, and in-between her escape attempts she had an opportunity to check out these other students and they didn't look so scary after all. She sat for several minutes, and after another escape attempt, though a feeble one, she remained quiet.

I stood behind her at a safe distance and was ready. What was she going to do? I waited and waited, but there she sat. Half an hour later I opened the door and made my exit. During recess, I returned to the class and the teacher. The students had been released to the playground and the substitute was preparing for the next instructional part of the day. She smiled: "Everything is going fine. In fact she has made a friend. The two of them are now playing on the yard."

Not only had Olivia remained in class, she had made a friend. In the world of elementary school students where social adjustments are so important, one friend can make the difference between a successful adjustment or a non-public school placement. I went to the playground and the sandbox where Olivia and her friend were playing. They laughed, they giggled, and for the two of them everything was exactly as it should be. And it was as though Olivia, our "psychotic, sexually abused, emotionally disturbed girl," who could only be successful in an expensive non-public school for the psychotic, was suddenly like every other student within the school. She was playing with a friend and was happy.

Olivia was my first case as I began my career as a school psychologist and she made a successful adjustment for the remainder of that school year. Months later when I thought back about what had happened it all seemed so easy. Olivia and this modification experience actually went much smoother than I had originally thought. Just follow the guidelines for behavior modification, as all the college professors described, and the desired results will follow. But, of course, you also have to be willing to make a few unsuspected adjustments along the way.

That was how it all began and I remained in those five schools for only this one semester. The following year I was transferred to another part of the city. For me, Olivia's story had come to an end and she and I would never again see each other. We had battled it out and as a result we both came out winners.

CHAPTER 6

WELCOME TO GARFIELD HIGH SCHOOL

NOW GO AWAY!

It was at Lincoln High School where I had felt the most satisfaction and where I believed my individual counseling skills could be most useful. I had gained experience and confidence in talking with students not only individually, but also in running group counseling. I even had what I believed to be one of the first entirely gay and lesbian counseling groups in the city. This was at a time when schools were reluctant to admit they had gay and lesbian students on their campuses. The group was my secret. I'd also dealt with every kind of adolescent difficulty possible: suicide, physical and sexual abuse, gangs and drugs. It was at Lincoln where I felt I could best use my skills and where I felt most needed. After several years of working within the elementary schools, I decided I would transfer to a high school and I was accepted into the High School Division shortly after this.

The first meeting of the new school year, always held after Labor Day, was the traditional kick-off meeting that brought us back from those lazy days of summer. The adjustment was always difficult on this first day, but for several of us this meeting brought an extra amount of tension. Of the fifty senior high school psychologists, about fifteen were being changed from a previous high school or, as was my case, we were being given our first assignment. A coordinator was in charge of making these placement decisions and he was in no hurry to let us know what our school assignment was going to be. Time dragged on. We heard announcements from the school's superintendent and also from the president of the Board of Education. My only concern was where I would be assigned.

Finally, the coordinator went to a small table to the side of the auditorium. He sat down and pulled a stack of letter-sized envelopes from a glistening jet-black attaché case. He looked out to the auditorium and began calling us to his table. One by one each of the various psychologists marched forward. The coordinator then slowly gave this person the envelope with their assignment. I watched and waited.

After all of the others had received their assignments, he called out my name: "Richard Selby." He looked to the audience and saw me getting up from my seat and coming forward. I approached the table and could feel my heart pounding. The Los Angeles Unified School District extends from Woodland Hills in the San Fernando Valley all the way to San Pedro, and from West Los Angeles to East Los Angeles. It comprises something like six hundred square miles and there are fifty high schools. Would I be sent many miles from home? Would it be my destiny to be stuck on some freeway with the millions of others who have to travel them each day?

"I'm giving you Garfield High School," he said. "Welcome to Garfield High School and the High School Division."

This felt so good and at last I knew my assignment.

"It has had a few problems last year, but I am sure you can handle it."

His eyes turned away and I went back to my seat. He was done and we had all now received our schools. I would be working in East Los Angeles and my drive would not be what I had feared. At long last my dream had come true. I would once again be working in a high school.

Later at break time, Harvey von Stuck, one of the more senior of the school psychologists, approached me. He shook his head: "You've been given Gina's old school and she had a very hard time there. That administration has a reputation for being difficult. They threw Gina out. And the community surrounding the school has many problems: gangs, violence, drugs, and poverty. It is a very hard school to work at."

Several minutes later I was introduced to Gina. She was on the short side and slightly rotund. She told me that she had worked at Garfield for the past three years, but five months into the last school year she had been thrown out: "I was told they didn't want me and that I had been a troublemaker. The kicked me off the campus and I was placed at the area office where I spent the remainder of the year. The coordinator told me I could never return to Garfield. But I didn't back down from any of them. They're a bunch of male-machos over there who think they can just push women around. Well, I showed them there are some women they can't push around."

Gina was proud that she had taken these strong stances and that she'd stood up to what she felt was an unfair administrative system at Garfield. "I'd do this again," she stated. "They're all a bunch of macho male bastards."

Once her position was vacated no other psychologist was sent to the school as a full time replacement. A substitute had reported intermittently, but he had done only a minimal amount of the mandated duties. This meant there was a tremendous backlog of work, but I was ready. Where Gina had run into problems, I was confident I would make an easy transition. And why should I think otherwise? After all, my previous principals had all marveled about what a good job I'd done and how they could rely on me to meet the needs of the school. After this first day of meetings, I would travel to Garfield the next morning.

I woke early and was excited. I drove to Garfield feeling the exhilaration that comes with beginning a new assignment. From home it was only about a twenty-minute ride to the school. With my heart pounding, I climbed the outside stairs and was inside the building where two ladies greeted me. They had a clipboard with several sheets of paper. "Where are you going?" the first one asked. The second followed up with, "Who is it that you want to see?" I explained and signed their papers. I climbed the stairs to the second floor and proceeded directly to the main office. A secretary came over.

"I'm the new psychologist. May I talk with the principal?"

I wanted to introduce myself to him, but for some reason she seemed quite surprised and didn't respond. After about fifteen seconds, she turned and went through a door that led directly to the principal's office. I looked around and could see that this was just another typical school office: teachers' mailboxes and a public telephone. Several minutes later a man approached and it was clear he was in a hurry. Part of his white shirt was tucked in while another part flopped loosely in back. He came directly towards me and squared his body on the opposite side of the counter. His eyes met mine and he turned sideways. He did not introduce himself, but I knew who he was.

"We don't have any special education students here at Garfield," he began. He had a cold stare and when he was sure that he had my fullest attention and that he wouldn't be misunderstood, he continued: "In this whole school we don't have any special students. We don't need a psychologist. You can go."

I pulled my assignment papers out of my pocket and placed them on the counter where they rested between the two of us. These were the official papers from my coordinator indicating that at Garfield High School there were four different special education classes. One of these classes was for students who were retarded. He pushed them to the side and squared his body with mine.

"There's been a mistake. We don't need a psychologist."

He returned to his office. This was not the way it was supposed to be. I'd lasted a total of ten minutes at my new school, but it was clear that my assignment had come to an abrupt end. It was good-bye Garfield High School.

CHAPTER 7

I'M A GARFIELD BULLDOG

"We don't have any special education students. We don't need a psychologist."

What was he talking about? All public schools have special education students. And this is not just in California, but also throughout the nation. Didn't he know? His shirt flopped as he returned to his office.

After about a minute, I returned my assignment papers to the white envelope and began retracing my steps, going down the stairwell to the ladies stationed at the entrance. I signed the appropriate spot on their clipboard indicating I had accomplished whatever it was that had brought me here and that I was now leaving. I went out the door and down the exterior steps. The temperature, which was hot when I'd arrived, now felt even hotter.

What should I do now? I unlocked the car, rolled down the window and started up the engine. *What kind of a man is this principal? Doesn't he know the laws? What was it that I had done that had provoked such a strange and unexpected response?*

I pulled my car onto the street and headed to the area offices to see my senior psychologist. She was the first person in the psychologist's chain of command for dealing with any problems that we might encounter.

It was a fifteen-minute drive and I wondered on this drive back what I would tell my immediate supervisor. It was clear that he didn't want me. And when I tried to show him my assignment papers he'd taken an angry stance and his lip turned up. He meant what he said. I was not wanted.

Fifteen minutes later I pulled into the parking lot at the downtown offices of the high school division. I went through a long hallway leading to Mary Stephenson's office. She was a senior psychologist. It was her responsibility to fix the problem, and if she could not, she would take it to the coordinator.

I made my way down the narrow hallway and stood at the door of her office. Actually it was just a cubbyhole and it was filled with psychological testing materials, psychological write-ups of students, books, and a variety of other odds and ends. It was jammed to the ceiling with all of these things and there was not an inch of space anywhere. Mary was busy at work and didn't notice as I stood there. I gently knocked to get her attention and she turned to me. This first day of real work wasn't half over and already one of the school psychologists had returned with a problem. I looked at my watch and it wasn't even ten in the morning.

Pushing the paperwork to one side, "What's wrong?"

I took several deep breaths.

"Slow down. What's going on?"

"The principal told me they don't have special education students. He said that within the whole school he doesn't have even one special education student. He told me that he doesn't want me. He doesn't need me and he told me to leave."

She moved her chair back and forth; the tiny wheels squeaked. "They don't want me!" I said again.

"That's garbage!" And I could hear her saying under her breath: "Total idiots!" And to me: "Where do we get these people? One of those classes is for retarded students. Doesn't he know that they're retarded? Does he think none of his students have learning difficulties? She hesitated momentarily and then, "They all think they can do whatever they want. I can't believe these high school principals."

She "jimmied" her chair, wheels squeaking, to the doorway and I stepped back. She stuck her head out. She looked down the hallway to the coordinator's office. He was the one with the power. She quickly turned back. There was a long line that had already formed at his door. Day one of psychological services within the schools was just getting underway, but already there were others who desired his attention. She scooted her chair back. Dealing with me and with a principal who wanted to defy the law had suddenly become her responsibility.

"I don't care what he says, he's wrong! It's your school and they have to take you. They have four special education classes. The law says they have to have a psychologist. They haven't had anyone there to complete the testing for much of last year, and the testing is way out of compliance."

I knew what she was thinking: *Why do I have to deal with such an irrational and poorly thought-out action by the principal? This is absolutely ridiculous. The action from this man doesn't make any sense.*

"They think they can do whatever they want over there," and she thought for a moment. "Well, they can't! Take the rest of the day off and go back tomorrow. They have to take you and they know it!"

Taking the rest of the day off was exactly what I was hoping she would say. I was frustrated, upset, and wanting to get started at my school. If I wasn't there, there was nothing for me to do.

The following day, as instructed, I arrived at Garfield High School and parked in the same spot. Unfortunately, the enthusiasm

I had felt on the previous day had waned considerably. I crossed the street and entered the building. I met the same two ladies at the entrance and signed their clipboard and went up the stairs. Would today be any different? I stood at the wooden counter and the secretary came over. She stood on the opposite side of the wooden counter and reached out to shake my hand: "Mr. Selby, it's nice to have you with us. You're now a Garfield Bulldog."

"You're now a Garfield Bulldog." Words I would never forget.

It was early September in 1985 and my desire to have a high school had come true. I had just turned forty and was looking for a place where I would remain for many years. Garfield High School, this school in East Los Angeles, would become my home for the next sixteen years.

One of the first teachers I met was a man by the name of Jaime Escalante. I met him during nutrition when the classes officially began. He wore a cap on his head and he taught math. Jaime Escalante was not outwardly impressive, at least not by the way he looked, but he exhibited self-confidence and he had earned the respect of both the teachers and the administrators. I wondered if this somewhat average looking man was the teacher I'd read about several months earlier in the morning paper. Could this Jaime Escalante really be the person who was having such great success in teaching calculus and who was getting so much publicity?

Well, it turned out that this Jaime Escalante and the man I was reading about in the papers were one and the same. Within several years he was destined to become world famous. In 1988, Hollywood would make a move about him and it was called "Stand and Deliver." It was nominated for an Oscar and our school in East Los Angeles suddenly became famous. Garfield was also visited by a variety of well-known people, including the soon-to-be president of the United States, George Bush, Sr.

CHAPTER 8

COURAGE UNDER FIRE

PART ONE

The administrators at Garfield decided that they liked me. Soon, with the support of Lee Patterson, who was in charge of the Drop-out Prevention Program, I was able to provide the direct kind of psychological services that Garfield needed: group counseling, working with teachers, counselors and students, and dealing with all types of emergencies. Then the school's principal decided that he wanted even more of my time. He was supportive and added to my duties. While most school psychologists were primarily involved with special education and their assessments, I was providing the full range of psychological services.

It was February, several years after I'd begun at Garfield and it was a strange time. I sat in my office. *What is going on?* That normal flow of student emergencies, teacher and counselor referrals, and self-referrals from students had stopped. Not one student or teacher had inquired about my services for three days, three whole days. In a school of four thousand plus students, it was uncommon for me to go one day, or even one morning or afternoon without an emergency of some type. *Had all these students, along with the teachers and counselors, forgotten that I existed? Had they forgotten that they had a school psychologist?*

Whenever I found myself not dealing with the many crises that were the main part of my job, I did "catch up," completing those necessary psychological evaluations. "Testing is what is important," the coordinators said. "Complete those cases. We need to be in compliance!"

I had always been able to stay in compliance by completing most of the write-ups at home, but this week my life had changed. I was spending most of my working hours testing students and writing reports. I moved in my swivel chair to the large widow overlooking the street below and looked out to the neighborhood. I stretched my arms high and squinted my eyes. I yawned and then it came... "ring, ring, ring."

I picked up the phone: "Dick Selby," I responded.

"Hello, Dick. This is Ken Easum from Monterey."

This was a familiar voice. Dr. Ken Easum was the principal at our continuation school, Monterey High School. I provided services to Monterey's students just as I did at Garfield. Monterey had approximately seventy students, the majority of whom had been unsuccessful at Garfield. This school took some of our most unsuccessful students, those that had been projected to be dropouts and worked closely with them. There were some students that I'd worked with at Garfield that I later worked with when they transferred to Monterey. And it was also the case that there were some of Easum's students that I'd never worked with at Garfield, but I would work with them sometime after their arrival at Monterey.

It was a smaller school adjacent to the Garfield campus and it was a school that I loved. Dr. Easum and I had it worked out that if there were some type of emergency, I would go over to Monterey and help.

"Yes, Ken, what can I do for you?"

I appeared to be a calm, but inwardly I could feel my excitement building. I only received phone calls from him when there was something important.

"Can you come over and talk with a boy? He's really having some problems. I talked with him for awhile, but I think he needs to talk with you. Two nights ago he was working his job at a liquor store and it was robbed. The robbers killed one of his fellow workers and he's having a tough time dealing with this."

I listened, but did not respond. Though it was true I wanted to get away from this boredom in which I had found myself, what Dr. Easum was talking about was someone who had been killed.

"He looks really bad," Ken continued. "He looks like he hasn't slept all night. In fact, I don't think he has slept since it happened and that was two days ago. He's white as a ghost. I tried talking with him, but I'm not the expert." Ken stopped momentarily. Was he making his request as clear as it needed to be to ensure that I completely understood? And then, "He really needs to talk with you."

"I'll be right over. It'll take about ten minutes."

Was there ever a doubt? We both knew I'd be there. I hung up the phone, closed the two doors leading into my office and started off. Though the walk to the continuation school takes only five minutes, there was a certain protocol that needed to be followed. It was necessary for me to inform the secretaries about my off campus visitation. In less than a minute I was at the main office. "Becky," I called out, "they have an emergency at Monterey. I'll be there for awhile."

Becky was occupied with one of many tasks that her job as the school's head secretary demanded. But just as I was about to call out a little louder, I heard, "Okay Mr. Selby," and she continued with her work. She never turned to look at me but as always she was in tune with everything that happened in this office. Becky was my favorite. Then it was down the stairs and out the front doors. The sun was shinning brightly it felt good just being outside. I went down the block and turned the corner. Soon I arrived at Monterey's main office and went in. Dr. Easum stood behind the counter in a slightly bent over position; he was talking with Emilio. Easum's eyes met mine, but almost immediately they turned downward. And, instead of being his normal verbose and jovial self, Ken was surprisingly quiet.

"This is Emilio," he began. "I didn't exactly get the story right." He feigned a smile. "No," he said apologetically, "it didn't happen quite the way I told you," and that was all. His eyes motioned for Emilio and I to proceed into the adjacent room where it was customary for me to talk with these students.

It was an unorthodox beginning and I found myself wondering what it was that Ken Easum might have told me that was incorrect. Emilio and I entered the room. As we walked in I could see that Emilio was approximately six feet tall and on the slim side, probably weighing around one hundred fifty pounds. He wore brown shorts, the kind that probably began as long pants, but had been trimmed into shorts at some later date. These shorts came halfway down his legs, stopping at the knee joint. He wore black nylon socks that reached about three-quarters of the way up the calves. A baseball cap covered his head and it was pulled down and turned backwards.

Emilio moved slowly, keeping his head down, and just as Ken had indicated during our phone conversation, there was a definite lethargy to his manner. It was obvious that whatever it was that he had experienced affected him greatly and that he had not in any way recovered. I closed the door and went to the little table that was available for us. I sat down, but Emilio, rather than sitting in the wooden chair in the normal position, turned it backwards and let his arms dangle like lifeless vines over the back section of the chair. His head remained down and there was very little body movement.

As I looked at him I wasn't sure how to begin. Probably this was related to the manner in which he was acting. So I sat there quietly and looked around. Though I'd been in this room many times, I'd never taken the time to notice what it was really like. It was just an enclosure, a sectioned off portion of a portable bungalow that the school utilized for both an office and a kind of spare room. There were no windows. When the one door leading in to this smaller section was closed the air circulation came to a standstill. On hot days, and today was developing into one such day, it could become unbearable. Emilio's arms dangled, but slowly and with jerky movements he lifted his arms. A grimace came across his face.

"What happened?"

There was no response.

I asked a second time: "What happened?"

Again there was no response. My eyes moved away from Emilio back to the room. There was a small refrigerator and some other items: a microwave, a computer, a sink, and a faucet. Off to the other side there was a couch and a chair. The only sound was the hum of the refrigerator. Emilio's head remained down. I waited, but then...

"I shot. I killed. I shot. I killed."

CHAPTER 9

COURAGE UNDER FIRE

PART TWO

"I shot. I killed. I shot. I killed."
His voice was muffled, but I heard.
"I shot. I killed. I shot. I killed."
My body tightened while my stomach suddenly contracted. This definitely was not what Ken had told me.
"We were told not to go outside, but he would always go outside."
Couldn't Easum have gotten this one detail correct?
Emilio struggled and wanted to continue, but he was unable. He had become involved in a world that he didn't recognize and

that he didn't want. His head went down while he clinched the sides of the chair. After about thirty seconds, his head came up:

"I work with an Indian guy and we were closing up. I work at a liquor store in South-Central, Watts. We had just closed up and the Indian guy went outside to work on his scooter. He always does that, but the boss has told him a hundred times to lock the door behind him. He didn't. He never does. He left the door slightly open and went outside to work on his scooter. These three guys came and grabbed him and rushed into the store. I was inside and could see what was happening."

While he described the events he was pulled back into the experience. He was caught between wanting to talk and tell his story, and not being sure that he was capable of doing so.

Finally, "The officer said it was probably because I'd been shot before. That was why I reacted as I did. That is why I killed him. I think that is why I did it, too."

Shot before? Couldn't Easum have at least gotten one of these details right? My stomach knotted. This was not in any way what I had prepared myself for emotionally. Emilio stopped talking while the incessant hum of the refrigerator droned on. Finally, I asked: "Why had you been shot?"

Eye contact was non-existent: "In July, I was coming home from work when my car got rear-ended by a truck. We both got out of our cars and I could see that some damage was done. This other guy, an African-American, didn't want to talk with me, but instead got back into his truck. He was going to drive away. I was really mad and jumped into the back of his truck and he took off. While he was driving I was in the back calling him names and hitting at the rear window. He pulled into an ally and stopped. He got out of the truck and I stood up in the back. I looked at him and said, 'What's up?'

This "What's up?" statement is normally done simultaneously with the hands in front of the individual and with the palms turned upwards. This is not a question, but is actually a challenge.

"We stood there looking at each other. He pulled out a gun, a nine-millimeter; I was looking at him and he shot me. I couldn't believe it. I wasn't doing anything and he shot me. I fell out of the truck and he drove away. I crawled to the street and passed out. Some people found me. I don't remember what happened after that. They said I almost died. I was taken to the hospital, but didn't wake up until three days later."

Emilio raised his shirt. A scar covered the entire front portion of his stomach; it was between twelve to sixteen inches long and quite thick.

"I'm not going to let myself be shot again," and he pulled his shirt back down to where it hung loosely over his brown shorts. "I'm not going to let it happen again. I woke up in the hospital and didn't even know how I got there. I almost died. The officer said that is why I did what I did. He said that is why I killed him."

Nothing that I had heard up to this point made any sense and who was this student who I was talking with? Was Emilio a gang member? I didn't think so. His pants weren't baggy and his shirt wasn't excessively large. He wasn't wearing a "Raider" shirt, frequently indicting some type of gang involvement.

The quiet returned as the two of us sat and my thoughts turned from what he was saying and what he'd experienced to the veterans who'd returned from Vietnam. It had been more than twenty years since that war had ended, but some of these veterans could still be seen on the streets of Los Angeles. Veterans who continued to suffer from the war and from the emotional trauma they had experienced.

Emilio: "My friend had gone out to work on his motor scooter. That's when they came up to him. I could see what was happening as I looked through the window. That was when I grabbed it. It was on the shelf underneath and I took the gun out. I didn't know what I was going to do with it, but I had it. I knew I was ready. They came through the front door and I had the gun in my hand."

He adjusted his cap and tightened his black socks, pulling them higher on each leg. "They didn't have to keep coming. They could see that I had a gun, but all three kept coming. They had their heads covered with nylon stockings. I was behind the counter and there's an open space where we give people what they've bought. It's a fairly large space with enough room for someone to crawl through."

"One of them came through the crawl space while another came around and through the security door that my friend left open. The guy that came through the crawl space saw my gun was pointed right at him. He saw. He didn't have to keep coming, but he did. And then the other one who was coming around from the door came at me. He saw. They both could see that I had a gun. The one that came through the crawl space jumped at me. I shot him. I shot him in the stomach. He was down and the other one came at me. I held the gun on him. I didn't want to shoot."

Emilio's body tensed.

"I had the gun on him when the third guy came through the door. He had my friend and was holding his gun on him, right at my friend's head."

Emilio demonstrated how the gun was being held. It was pointed directly at the temple of his friend.

"And he kept saying, 'Give me the gun, mother fucker. Give me the gun,' and I wouldn't do it. I was so angry. I didn't want to get shot again. I didn't want to get shot again. I knew what'd happened before and I couldn't go through it again."

He became silent. He grabbed the sides of the chair.

"I had my gun on him and he had the gun right at my friend's head. That's when the other one came at me. I shot him. He fell to the ground. The one with the gun had this weird expression on his face. He kept looking at me. We just stood there and he kept yelling, 'Give me your gun, mother fucker, give me your gun. I'm going to kill him. Give me your gun,' but I wouldn't do it. I was looking right at him and I pointed my gun at his head and I was going to shoot. I was going to shoot that *chingada madre* (mother fucker) but I didn't want to shoot. I was afraid I'd hit my friend."

What this Monterey High School student was describing was the reality of battle. If he had been in Vietnam, World War I or World War II, he would be a hero. He would have been given a medal, but he wasn't in the army or in any type of war. He was an eighteen year old who'd been working at a liquor store to help support his mother and four siblings.

"Give me your gun, give me your gun," the remaining guy screamed, "or I am going to kill your friend." But I refused. I kept my gun pointing directly at this guy's head.

It was taking time, but Emilio was getting his story out and that was what was important. I also knew that there are times in life when everything seems unreal. As a protective mechanism we put up a shield and block ourselves from what had happened. Emilio had put up his shield, but now it was coming down.

"Everything was happening so fast. The two guys who I'd shot were on the ground. The first one tried to get up and run out of the store. I told him to stop and he tried to get by the guy with the gun. I was so angry that I went kind of crazy. That's what the policeman said, 'I went crazy.' I shot him as he tried to leave. He didn't get past the others and fell to the ground. I killed him. The other guy kind of freaked and kept yelling, 'Give me your gun! Give me your gun! I'm going to shoot him mother fucker. I'm going to shoot him. Mother fucker give me your gun.' We stood there looking at each other. He had his gun on my friend and I pointed my gun straight at his head. I wanted to pull the trigger and I'm a good shot. I used to practice at the target range, but I was afraid I'd hit my friend. He just kept yelling and I know I was crazy. This other guy knew I was crazy too. After that I don't exactly remember what happened. He pulled my friend with him and tried to get out of the store. He ran out of the store and I shot at him. I don't know for sure what happened except that I didn't hit him. I ran out of the store and saw him running away and I shot again. I kept shooting but was out of bullets. I had used all of them and I was still trying to shoot. The liquor store was a mess and there was blood all over the place. There were two guys still in the store. They were on the floor and one was dead."

There, it was out. Emilio had told his story and all I was able to do was sit. The reality of what he had experienced had overcharged my system. And what could I say to someone who had been involved in a true-to-life shoot out?

With my brain feeling the strain, I felt a kind of numbness. Was I, too, retreating in a minor sort of way from the world as I knew it? Emilio's baseball cap remained backwards and his nylon socks remained high on his calves. His head faced down while drops of sweat dripped off my forehead. *Here I am this professional,* I thought, *and I need to say something, but what?* The professional language that encompasses the field of psychology and that comes to the rescue of the well-trained clinician eluded me. And it wasn't just a loss of language. Time came to a standstill and we just sat. Suddenly my mind reactivated and a light switched on. I was ready.

"Emilio. His head was down. "You didn't want to be in this situation. You didn't ask for it, but they were the ones who came at you. You made it clear from the beginning you had a gun. You didn't shoot right away. You hesitated. You gave each of them time to see, to think about what they were doing, and most importantly to leave. They had time to turn and go out the door." I spoke slowly. "They didn't have to keep coming. Each one of them, making the decision for himself, could have stopped and left the store. They had the opportunity and if they had left right then, nothing would've happened. Each saw your gun. Each had the choice and each could simply have turned around and left." I emphasized, "They had every reason to leave, but didn't."

I looked at him and he was paying close attention.

"It was a horrible, terrible, awful situation for you to be in, and you didn't want this to happen. You didn't ask for it to happen. You didn't want them to come at you, but by your actions you probably saved your friend's life and your own."

Click! Those hands grasping the sides of the chair retracted and moved to the top section. His head came up and this stare, the one that represented the emotional wasteland where people go when they retreat from existence and from the world, had changed. Click, click, click. His eyes lit up.

"That's what the police told me. They said I was acting in self-defense. If I hadn't done anything, they might have killed all of us."

I knew this was true. Several months earlier I'd talked with another student who'd been working at a grocery store three blocks from Garfield. She was sixteen and was at the cash register. A man came into the store and told her to give him all of the money, and she did exactly as she was told. Her boss who was standing right next to her also told her to give him the money. For no reason at all, this man shot and killed her boss. This man, the robber and now murderer, looked at her and pointed this gun at her head. He held it within two feet of her head and he was going to pull the trigger. But for some reason and with her boss dead on the floor, he pulled the gun away and walked out. I had talked with her just as I was talking with him.

I was sure that these three men who had come into Emilio's liquor store were criminals and possibly murderers. They'd robbed in the past and they may have even killed. These men were dangerous and they were armed, and they were prepared to use their weapon. I emphasized to Emilio: "You were in a horrible situation. These three men had robbed other stores before coming into yours. They knew what they were doing and they'd planned it out. If you had done anything different than what you did, they'd have killed you. They'd have killed your friend, but you were there. You didn't ask to be there, but you were." And, "Each of them had an opportunity to leave. They saw your gun. They had a choice. They could have turned around and walked out."

These words were soothing and helped, but my words were dulled by the nightmare through which he had lived. It had only been two days, but for the first time his eyes made contact and he looked at me.

"That's what they told me. There was nothing that I could do and I just kind of panicked. There was blood all over the place. One of them is in the hospital and one is dead. The other one got away."

Emilio had been challenged in a way that few of us will ever be challenged, and he had reacted with courage. Emilio, this skinny eighteen year-old with thin white legs, black nylon socks and a baseball cap turned backwards, had met the most difficult obstacle that could be faced in life. Emilio didn't back away and confronted it head on.

"You're going to need time to recover. I don't know how much time, but you've had a terrible experience and it will take your mind and your body time to get through it. I believe you need to continue in counseling. We've several places near the school where you can go. I'll leave the information with Dr. Easum. I also believe that in your entire life you may never experience anything more difficult than what you have just been through. Yes, this will take time, but you are going to return to normal."

We rose from our chairs and started out. Emilio wasn't cured, but he'd told his story and in this world of conflict, tragedy, love, death, heartache and the unexpected, it's the telling of the story that is most important. It's people curing themselves and the willingness to confront life's problems that moves them back to health. Courage is needed. Courage is what separates those who will successfully adjust from those who won't. One thing Emilio had was courage. We exited the room to the central office where Dr. Easum was waiting. Emilio went outside to the other students and his friends.

"How's he doing?" Easum asked. "It wasn't what I told you."

"No, it wasn't." I hesitated, and then…"He's having a hard time."

Ann, the office manager and secretary, came over. She could see that this conference had been very difficult: "Well, you look like you could use a coke and some cookies," and with this she handed me an ice-cold coke and a few of her homemade chocolate chip cookies. Ann was the greatest and she had the deepest understanding of life. In times of stress revert to the basics, junk food, and within minutes our conversation had returned to normal.

"How's Garfield?" Ken asked.

"Same old, same old. Still got students."

"That's good. Still got the boss lady?"

"Still got her."

We both laughed. I chomped a few cookies and gulped the coke. My body responded to the rush of sugar and the shot of caffeine. The surest sign that I'd recovered was the return of my sense of humor. And Emilio, well he, too, was on the road to recovery. He was outside shooting hoop. I watched him for a minute and knew he was one of the toughest individuals I'd ever met. He grabbed the ball taking it high. He shot and made a basket. There's nothing like a little basketball to really "therapize" someone and get him back on the right track.

The sun was hot with not a cloud on the horizon, and Monterey was such a pretty little school. It even had its own miniature golf course. Money was donated from businesses in the area for the materials and the students built it themselves. *I love coming over here,* I thought. *Why don't we have more schools like this?* Students sat under picnic tables eating their lunches and this one day of summer was upon us. I took a last deep breath and basked in the glory of the moment, but the time had come to return to the larger school.

"Got to go. Got paperwork waiting for me at Garfield."

"Sure," Easum responded, "that'll be the day that you do paperwork." Ann also acted as though she couldn't believe it with an upward movement of her eyes. Well, that was how it went. Ken didn't believe me about paperwork and Ann just shrugged her shoulders and moved her eyes in a manner to show that she, too, didn't believe my story. This statement about paper work could only be another of my fabrications, but we all knew it was time for me to be getting back to the other school, the larger school with its thousands of students.

"Good-bye," I said, and I again thanked Ann for the cookies and coke. "Adios, Ken," and I was gone, out the gate, up the block, around the corner and through the large external doors that led into the fifth largest high school in the nation, Garfield High School. Then it was up one flight of stairs to the main office.

"Becky," I called out. "I'm back."

"Oh, Mr. Selby, there are some messages for you. And Mr. Jolon (the head counselor) says you need to talk with a student. It's an emergency."

"Thanks, Becky."

Three whole days had gone by with only testing. Three days of test, test, test, score, score, score, and write, write, write. Not one emergency, not one pregnancy, not one boyfriend-girlfriend squabble, no one crying in the classroom, but now I was needed. I picked up my messages from my mailbox, talked with Mr. Jolon and walked up the remaining flight of stairs to my office, but Emilio and what he had experienced was still on my mind. He was tough and his name seemed fitting. It was Emilio, just like Emilio Zapata who had been a leader in the Mexican revolution. And this Emilio from Monterey High School had proven his mettle. Did these robbers have any idea what they had gotten themselves in for when they went into that liquor store? How could they possibly have known? I reached the top stair and turned the corner when I saw two students standing by my door.

"Where have you been?" they asked in unison. "We need to talk with you." One was in tears.

Yes, with Garfield there were always problems. I unlocked the door and the two rushed in. I asked them to sit down and I, too, sat down. But before I could begin getting any information about why they needed to see me, the phone rang. It was Edy Dunlap, one of our social studies teachers.

"Richard," she began, "I've got an emergency." She was desperate. "Can I send her over? You need to talk with her right away."

"Sure, send her over."

One of the two girls who'd been waiting for my return could no longer restrain herself: "Oh, Mr. Selby you're not going to believe what happened," and my life at this inner city school had returned to normal. Five minutes later the other student arrived. I asked her to have a seat and to be patient. Counseling takes time and she would have to wait. No, it wasn't total privacy that my office provided, but the two other girls didn't mind. They knew that this office was a safe haven and that students who were experiencing problems could come at just about any hour. It was all confidential, for those of us who were in the room, but I would provide the privacy that a particular student might need when such privacy was important. Counseling in room 436 was again in session.

That was the way it went from that day onward. Never again was I to experience even one day without some type of emergency. It was boyfriend-girlfriend issues, suicide, abuse, drugs, and gay and lesbian concerns. We had gangs and the violence of the barrio, and it was all with us as a part and parcel of the Garfield experience. And to add to the excitement in its own way, California, and for this one calendar year, went from a drought to wintry rains, and to one blissfully hot summery day.

The following days I again found myself overloaded with crises and I knew the truth. Paperwork isn't so bad; I just wished I had the time to get it done.

Several months later and just as the school day had ended, I ran into my two friends, Ken Easum and his office manager Ann. They had come to Garfield to use the equipment in one of the smaller offices. Ann was typing while Ken stood next to her. He was doing what he did best, supervising.

"Yo, Ken," I screeched as I peeked into their office. I enjoyed running into the two of them. "What brings you over to Garfield?"

Ken was looking over Ann's shoulder. He turned, "Oh, we have some work to do. Ann's working while I supervise."

My eyes caught Ann's. "Ann, I think you should make him do the work."

"R I G H T," she responded. "R I G H T," and she dragged out the entire word. We all knew what this answer meant. There was no hope of getting Dr. Easum to do any of the real work. It had been awhile since we had talked and I decided to ask: "Whatever happened to Emilio?" Was he successful? Had he recovered from the trauma?

Ann stopped her typing and sat quietly at her typewriter. She knew what was to follow and she wanted to see my reaction. A smile came across Easum's face and his mustache moved up and down and twitched. We both knew that something significant was about to be said.

"Oh, Emilio," Ken continued, "He's doing fine. And he's had a baby. Can you believe that? In one year he got shot, killed someone, and now he's had a baby."

"Yes," I responded, "that's pretty amazing."

Ann returned to her typing and Easum returned to his supervisory position. That school year came to a close and Emilio graduated from Monterey Continuation School. He received his diploma at a special graduation ceremony held for all the continuation school graduates throughout the district. Emilio, even through everything that he had experienced, became a high school graduate and a new father.

I was not to hear about Emilio again; I'd hoped I'd been a part of his recovery. But the students of Monterey High School, its principal, Dr. Ken Easum, and the secretary, Ann, and I were to work together for many years to come.

CHAPTER 10

ONE IN TEN

"Aha, aha, aha, aha!"

The laughter could be heard throughout the small room, into the hallway, out the window and to people standing two stories below. It was a bellowing, all-encompassing sound that echoed past the normal boundaries, but this was the way it was. This was Gary. When he laughed everyone and everything stopped in their tracks and you never knew when or where this outburst might happen. If he were in class, instruction would come to a standstill.

Ms. Sell, the drama teacher, had warned Gary about the problems he created when he laughed these attention-gathering guffaws. In drama, which was his favorite class, it could be ten minutes before the students calmed down. Ten minutes lost to restore order and getting the students to again focus on their work, only to have him do it again. These disruptions had reached a point of crisis in her class and if he didn't control himself, Ms. Sell was going to throw him out. She had provided sufficient warning and if he did not self-correct and soon, he would have to find another class.

Gary looked at Ms. Sell, upon receiving what he knew was his last warning: "I was born to act," he responded. "I don't live until I am on stage."

She knew this was true, but then this was her class: "There'll be no more loud outbursts or you're out."

The warning worked and Gary was able to modify his actions in her class. And as part of the process to reinforce this change she referred him to the school psychologist and to group counseling. Perhaps some sort of therapy might also be beneficial?

So that was the way it began. Gary became a member of Focus, the name for the weekly counseling groups. However, just as it had been with drama and with his other classes, Gary's behavior in the Focus group was at times problematical. His laughter was frequently cause for concern. Several of his friends, all of whom were girls, joined him in these groups, and when his behavior reached the point of disruption or annoyance, they would help him return him to a calmer state.

"Don't respond to what he says," Mercedes stated during one of the group sessions to the other members of the group. "Just relax. Don't pay any attention. He's had a very tough time recently and it's his way of letting off steam. He'll calm down in a minute and he'll be ready to participate. But don't react."

Of all of his friends, Mercedes was the most helpful and during these high school years she had become his closest confidant. Mercedes, seventeen years old and with long black hair, had developed this friendship with him when they were in junior high school. She knew Gary perhaps better than anyone else. And she had made a personal commitment to do everything that she could do to help him survive during these difficult years. Gary was the one in ten. He was gay, and along with this sexual orientation he was effeminate in his mannerisms. It was this combination of factors that made his adjustment to Garfield so difficult.

On this Tuesday in November, Mercedes was dealing with more than the normal adjustment problems. She turned and gave him a stern look: "Calm down, Gary!"

But when he did not calm down, and when he continued with what was clearly an unacceptable loudness, it was time to become more forceful: "Don't be a B-I-T-C-H." She spelled out the word "bitch," and looked him squarely in the eyes. She was forcing him to pay attention.

Gary shrugged his shoulders and his head came down: "I can't help it." His words were muffled. "If that's the way I am, that's the way I am. I just can't change myself to please people."

His eyes scanned the room as he looked at everyone. Yes, once again he had managed to become the center of attention. He turned to her.

"Yes, sometimes I am a bitch. But I also get tired of being pushed around. Sometimes I just have to be a bitch."

His head rested on Mercedes' shoulder. He cuddled close and caressed her hand. Mercedes, at least for the moment and for the beginning of this group session, had succeeded in modifying his behavior.

It was 1994 and being gay or lesbian, especially being gay, was reason enough for a student to be teased and taunted by other students. Over the past nine years I had worked with a variety of gay and lesbian students in my group and I'd talked with many individually, but Gary was different. His ostentatious behavior, along with his obvious gay orientation and effeminate mannerisms, made him an easy target for other students. Wherever he went, whether it was from one class to the next, or to lunch or nutrition, it was necessary for him to be accompanied by someone from his small group. Gary's very survival depended upon the protection these girls provided.

During this day in the Focus group, Mercedes was not only focused, but she had an agenda that she was going to adhere to. The way she saw it, Gary's weakness was in forming relationships... and in finding what he felt was his "significant other." Mercedes had known him for more than five years and knew his strengths and his weaknesses. She had come to understand his behavior and the patterns that she'd seen repeated time after time. Recently, he had become interested in another boy, a student who did not feel a similar attraction towards him.

"Gary," Mercedes said as she turned directly to him and with the sternest of looks, "you have to learn to control yourself. You can't always let your emotions and your feelings get in the way."

His hand caressed hers. He kept his head down and next to her shoulder.

She nudged him: "And Gary, you have to be careful with Hector. I think he is just playing with you."

Gary's eyes lit up. He raised his head: "But he's so cute." A smile crossed his face; he clasped her hand in his and slowly pulled it next to his chest. "I love the way he walks. I love his buns. Can't you tell him that I'll do anything for him? I'll be his sex slave. Oh, if only I could be his forever."

His words were spoken in a high pitch and the phrase was punctuated even higher when he concluded. Was he acting? Was he serious? It was hard to know and most of the time he himself may not have known, but one thing was for sure, he was flamboyant.

Gary also had a serious side. He was soft, gentle, intuitive, and he had a deep capacity for understanding emotions and the reasons behind someone's actions, but with this awareness came the paradox: even though he understood other people's emotions and why they acted as they did, and even though he had a good understanding of his own emotions, he was unable to modify his behavior.

Mercedes scolded him: "Gary, Hector is just playing you. He doesn't care about you. He knows that you will do anything for him."

"I will do anything for him," and Gary was serious. "He's everything I want in a man. He can use me and abuse me. I don't care, just so I have him."

In stature Gary was five feet-nine inches tall and weighed one hundred forty-five pounds. His hair was black and of medium length, but he was always well groomed. He had a penchant for dressing nicely. His skin was of an olive color.

"Gary!" Mercedes repeated, and she was at the point where she had to assert herself: "You have to protect yourself. If you don't protect yourself, no one else will." She was concerned that this new relationship, this new love of his, would die the same death as so many others had in the past.

Gary laid his head gently upon her shoulder, holding her hand tight. His voice was soft and his manner had now changed from loudness to softness: "I know. I know. You've told me that at least a hundred times, but I just never seem to listen." He snuggled. "You're so nice. You're always trying to protect me. That's sweet." His head rested comfortably upon her shoulder. Mercedes placed her head next to his. Finally Gary had calmed down and we proceed with the group.

I had met Gary three months earlier. While many of Garfield's students struggled with grades and failed a variety of classes, Gary did not. He had maintained a solid "B" average. During this his senior year, he was assigned to work sixth period, the last period of the day in the attendance office. For other students who received this assignment, it was supposed to be a fun class, an honor conveyed upon only the select few; and that's the way it was, except for Gary. Here was the problem: a major part of the assignment was to pick-up the attendance rosters at the end of the day from all of the other classes in the school. A simple task, but it was dangerous for Gary to walk alone, and he was unable to walk into many of the classrooms without being called names: gay, fag, and *maricon,* The attendance office had tried sending him to the various classes, but it had gotten to the point where many teachers had been emphatic with the administrators at this office: "Don't send him into the room. When he comes into the room it produces too many problems. It is very difficult to control the students."

Ellen, one of the clerks in this office, had personally witnessed these students' reactions when Gary entered various rooms.

"I can't send him out," she told me in confidence one afternoon. "It's impossible and I know he wants to go. He wants to be like everyone else, but it just does not work out. It's too dangerous for him to be alone out there. The assistant principal has given me specific instructions not to send him out. She's afraid that he'll be injured." So in the attendance office he remained. It was in this office where there were adults who could monitor what was going on and insure that nothing would happen. And if there was no work for him to do, he was expected to sit. During this sixth period class, he often could be seen sitting alone and bored while all of the other student workers were out performing the standard duties.

One day near the conclusion of the first semester, Gary was working in the attendance office.

"Mr. Selby, can I talk with you?"

I turned and he was just several feet from me, sitting on one of the large metal stools.

"Sure!"

He appeared to be worried and quite upset about something. I gathered the few items I had placed on the wooden counter next to me: "Let's go on up to the office." We went upstairs to the office and found some chairs. Gary was upset and immediately ready to begin.

"Love is awful. Love is horrible. The boy I want doesn't want me. I just don't know what to do?"

"Slow down, Gary. What are you talking about?"

"It's Hector." (This was the boy that Mercedes was concerned about during the group session.) "I know I can't have Hector, but I want him 'soooo' bad," as he emphasized the point. "And now I can't believe what I'm doing. I'm 'sooo' mean. Mr. Selby, I'm just terrible sometimes. I'm just using Douglas (another boy) for my sexual needs. I'm just using him. And I'm so mean to him. He's so much in love with me. He thinks I'm everything. His mother doesn't even know that he's gay. We sit there on the couch and all we can do is talk. She is always watching us. Then we have to sneak outside. And you know what bothers me the most?"

"No."

"He's only fourteen years old. I'm with a baby. It's so embarrassing. We don't have anything to talk about. He doesn't even know how to talk. We just sit there. I say something and he doesn't even know what to say. I'm so embarrassed."

Over the years I'd talked with many students and my conversation with Gary was the type of thing that I did with all students, heterosexual or gay. The gay students, just as the others, shared their concerns and their difficulties and I'd come to believe that gay or lesbian relationships did not differ in any significant way from those of heterosexuals. The only difference that I could discern had to do with the selection of the significant partner and that was all.

"But I'm the one who always gets hurt. And that's why I'm trying to hurt him. I've had it happen to me so many times and now I see myself trying to hurt him. He will do anything for me. He loves me so much. He says I'm everything to him and I just take advantage of him."

It was when he said this that I felt a tinge of discomfort. Gary was sharing extremely personal thoughts and actions, and at this moment it seemed strange. I wasn't gay, but he trusted me and that was enough. I looked around my office and could see pictures of other students who had also shared intimate details of their personal lives: relationship issues, love issues, physical abuse, sexual abuse, suicide ideation, and those others who shared concerns dealing with being gay or lesbian. Gary's words pulled me back.

"I want to be in control. I want to be the one in charge. I want to have one hundred percent control over what happens. When I'm in control then I know this other person can't hurt me."

"Does it work, being in control?" (The need to control is one of the most significant issues with which many people deal.)

He stopped and thought.

"Does having one hundred percent control protect you from getting hurt? Because you are in control does that mean that the other person will respect and love you more?"

He sat, thinking about this current relationship and the others that he'd been involved in. He'd had a countless number of relationships and yet he always ended up alone. Why wasn't he being successful, after all the attempts he'd made in meeting his someone special? And why was he always feeling disappointed about the relationship and about himself?

"No, it doesn't work. I know it doesn't work. Can you believe that? I know what I am doing will not bring me what I want and yet I do it. I'm too afraid to do anything else. I'm afraid that I won't be loved. When I'm in control I feel protected. I feel that I cannot be hurt, but I'm always afraid that no matter what I do, I'll be rejected." He stopped for a minute and thought: "I don't want to be rejected again. I need to be in control. It's my way of protecting myself. I want to control the other person. I want that other person to hurt, not me. I don't trust the other person so I want to be in control."

Trust, which is a most important part of a loving relationship, is difficult to maintain when there is an excessive need to control. Gary, in a sense, was trapped by his own emotions. He had also lived with tremendous emotional pain and rejection. Throughout his entire education, even when he was in kindergarten, he was identified by the other students and his teachers as someone who was different. Boys frequently picked on him and teased him. In junior high school the teasing had become worse, but it was also in junior high school when his life changed for the better. He made friends with Mercedes and several other girls. They helped protect him and now when he was a senior and in his final year at Garfield his problems hadn't ended. There was no place on the campus where he could safely walk without being teased and harassed. He had learned early that he was different and that he was an outcast. And all he really wanted was to find that loving relationship with another, his significant other. Would this ever happen? Only time would tell. But on this day having a compassionate ear to listen to him was what he needed.

He talked and I listened. When it was appropriate I shared with him the difficulties that everyone, including myself, had in finding that right person. "It takes time," I explained, "but you also are learning along the way." I encouraged him to be honest with himself and to continue to learn about himself. I stressed that he needed to evaluate each and every relationship as it progresses and that he needed to be honest with himself about how he felt about each one. "These things take time, but they're worth it."

And the bell rang ending the school day. Classes were over and his friends would soon be waiting. "Thanks," he said and he got up from his chair. "I feel better. You always make me feel better."

The day was over and with that final bell came a sense of relief. There would be no more emergencies and I could at last relax. Gary exited through the tiny hallway, turned and quickly mixed in with those other students leaving their classes. I sat for about a minute and then went to the window and watched below. I knew that it would be in the center of the grassy area where he and his friends would meet: Maria, Sharon, Mercedes and Juana, four adolescent girls with adolescent problems of their own. They all had boyfriends and their own relationships difficulties, but they had come together and taken on Gary. They were his protectors, his guardians.

I watched the group as it formed: one, two, three, four, and then Gary. Did any of them have a problem in the world, and was Gary in any way different from any other student here at the school? Yes, he was, but to them it didn't matter. They accepted him just as he was. I watched and as I sat there it came: "Aha, aha, aha," laughter careening to my office from three stories below.

Several days later the first semester came to an end. Students on the same track as Gary would take a well-deserved hiatus from school and wouldn't return until March. Gary turned eighteen during these next two months and decided that he'd had enough of

Garfield. He enrolled in the nearby community college and eventually earned his junior college degree. I was never to see him again, but Ms. Sell, the drama teacher, continued to keep in contact with him for many years.

CHAPTER 11

THE PAST PAYS A VISIT

One September in the mid-1990's a new school year was again upon us; but this year we were in for some big changes. District administrators decided that overcrowding was the issue to be dealt with, which we all knew was true in East Los Angeles. We simply had too many students and too few classrooms, especially in the elementary schools. Something needed to be done.

The solution was to send the sixth graders to the junior high schools, opening up space for the incoming students in the elementary schools. The junior high schools were reconfigured. They now had sixth graders, but they sent their ninth graders to the high schools. Garfield High School with this new alignment became a four-year high school and for us it was a rude awakening. It did not take long for our teachers, counselors and administrators to learn that ninth graders were not like the others. Ms. Shiroishi, the counselor for the computer-science magnet, came face to face with some of these additional problems.

"I can't believe these ninth graders," she blurted. Could anyone hear her? It didn't matter; she was at the end of her rope. She had temporarily lost her ability to handle those miniscule and incessant difficulties that had now occupied the major part of her job. "I can't believe them! They're all just babies."

This was not the Ms. Shiroishi that we all knew and loved. After all she was the best of the best, *la crème de la crème*. Joanne had been in this counseling position for the past twenty years, having graduated from college at the age of twenty. Immediately following her graduation she completed her teaching credential and began at Garfield. Several years later she became a counselor and her direct involvement with our students had become the passion of her life. But now the impossible had happened. The ninth graders, these neophytes into the world of high school, had gotten the best of her. She glared at the packed waiting room. Ninth graders almost all of them and occupying many of these seats were students she'd seen earlier in the day.

"Hi, Joanne," I whispered as I scooted by. I looked in to see her cubbyhole, labeled as an office, but I knew what was happening. "They're just babies," said it all.

Later that day Ms. Shiroishi stopped me as I was again walking through the counseling offices; she placed a referral in my hand: "Read it when you have time. Another of our ninth graders needs some help." Fifteen minutes later I opened her referral:

Dick,
I have a student that I would like to refer to you. Her name is Monica and she's been having some problems. She's not doing very well in her classes and she's very smart. She appears to be somewhat depressed. A support group might be beneficial. Can you talk with her?

Joann Shiroishi

From the looks of this referral, her request had the appearance of being just another of the minor referrals that so frequently passed my way. There seemed to be no impending possibility of suicide or of abuse, which of course would require my immediate attention. No, as I read her referral this was nothing special. Monica was simply another of our immature ninth graders feeling lost in the shuffle. I placed the referral on my desk and would get to it later that day. After lunch I wrote out the summons slip and took it to the attendance office where I had one of their service workers take it to her class. Within a matter of a few minutes, a skinny, long-haired ninth grader stood outside my outer door.

When she arrived I was seated at my table with my typical assortment of paperwork spread out. I turned my attention from my work to my little hallway and in she strolled. This was what had always happened in the past, but when I took a longer and more focused look something didn't seem right. The first image, which I now recognize as being the correct one, was of a tall, slim and smiling adolescent. Here was a young girl who had a pleasant way of presenting herself and who gave the impression of being quite comfortable around people. But as I watched all of this changed and I'm not sure exactly what it was that happened. Momentarily, I seemed to drift into a different emotional state and she reminded me of someone I had met somewhere in the past. Something wasn't right and I knew immediately that this was weird and unexpected. Both my mind and body reacted.

Monica, fortunately for me, was unaware of what I was experiencing and took a seat, patiently waiting for some type of official introduction. Finally, when at last I realized I needed to say something, I began: "I'm Dick Selby," and I reached out to shake her hand. "I've been asked to talk with you."

"I know. Ms. Shiroishi and I have talked several times and this morning she recommended that I talk with you."

Her eye contact was good, always an indication of sufficient self-confidence, but I continued feeling strange. Was I reacting this way because of something I had eaten?

"Why don't you tell me a little about yourself?" *Get on with this! You'll get over this temporary discomfort. Just keep going.*

I learned that Monica lived with her mother and that she had one younger brother, a half-brother, and there was a stepfather in the home. She didn't know where her natural father was and she had never seen him. She hoped someday to know him, but for now the stepfather was the problem.

"I don't like him," she began, "but I love my mother very much. She's wonderful."

Just as Ms. Shiroishi had indicated there appeared to be no risk of suicide or of abuse. Monica was what she was, simply another of our ninth-graders experiencing adjustment difficulties. In another year she'd be fine, but a little additional support for now could be helpful.

I explained the weekly groups that I ran and she let out a big smile. This was what she was hoping for, to join with others and discuss those important concerns about growing up. We agreed that I would call her home that very night. If mother were in agreement, then she could participate in one of the groups the following day. I told her that I would make the call at seven.

Things as so often happen didn't go the way I had anticipated. It was ten that night when I realized I'd not yet made this pre-arranged call. Monday Night Football was the culprit. My son and I watched as we each rooted for our favorite team and the victor was not decided until the last thirty seconds. His team won and it was getting late. It was time to go to bed, but as I did so I noticed a small yellow post-it that was stuck to the outside of my wallet.

"Oh no!" I blurted out loud, and I knew that I had forgotten all about this call. I immediately went to the phone and dialed the number. The phone rang several times and somebody answered it

"Hello," I said, "I'd like to speak with Mrs. -----. I'm Mr. Selby from Garfield High School."

A simple yes or no was all that I desired, but it wasn't going to be as easy as I had anticipated. The parent began screaming: "Mr.

Selby! This is Rosa! Mr. Selby! Rosa! Rosa! Don't you know me? This is Rosa!"

I thought, *Who is Rosa?* It was getting late and I needed to get to bed. I had no interest in dealing with an hysterical parent.

"Mr. Selby! This is Rosa! Don't you know me?"

No, I thought, *I do not know a Rosa, at least none that would be screaming at me at this hour of the night, and what difference does it make anyway? Yes or no is all I need for Monica to participate in the morning group counseling session! I'm tired.*

"This is Rosa, Mr. Selby!"

"Mrs. -----," I responded as I tried my best to remain calm, "I talked with Monica today and would like to try her in one of my support groups."

But no matter what I said it didn't help.

"Mr. Selby, this is Rosa!"

"Yes, I know," but I realized the truth. I was dealing with a parent who was having difficulties maintaining a normal mental state. I knew I'd better be careful with this one and proceed with caution. "I'm Mr. Selby from Garfield High School." I spoke slowly. "I'm the school psychologist. I'd like to talk with you about..."

"Mr. Selby, this is Rosa!"

Rosa? Rosa? Should I know someone named Rosa?

"Don't you know me?"

"I'm sorry, I do not."

"Mr. Selby, this is Rosa. This is Rosa Sanchez."

"I don't know a Rosa Sanchez."

"This is Rosa Sanchez from Lincoln High School! Mr. Selby, Rosa Sanchez from Lincoln High School. You know me. You have to know me."

Rosa Sanchez? What was it that she'd just said? Did she say that she was Rosa Sanchez from Lincoln High School? And those past twenty years seemed like only yesterday.

"Rosa Sanchez from Lincoln High School," I yelled. Now I was the one screaming. "Rosa Sanchez from Lincoln High School. I don't believe it! Rosa Sanchez from Lincoln High School."

I would never forget those experiences of Lincoln High School and of Rosa and her three childhood friends. It was in 1973 when I began working there as a grade counselor. It was a wonderful experience and during my first year students routinely invaded my office. But it was to be Rosa who had an encounter with three of the most dangerous *cholas* (gangster girls) on the Lincoln High School campus, as told in Chapter 2. I was to find Rosa one morning surrounded by three gangster girls and hundreds of other students. A riot was about to happen and I had become the person who was to handle this situation completely by myself.

Rosa and I talked about what had happened and we even laughed. It turned out to be something that neither of us would ever forget, and by the time our conversation ended I had obtained the necessary permission for Monica to join the group.

The following day Monica attended the group and everything went well. In fact everything went well for the next two months, but the day came when I received an emergency phone call: "Mr. Selby! This is Rosa Sanchez." (Rosa did not use her married name when we spoke.) "My daughter is having some serious difficulties and I'm very worried. Something bad, very bad is about to happen. I think it'd be best if I came in to talk with you about it. Can I come in tomorrow?"

At ten o'clock the following morning I heard a noise. I turned from my work to see a middle-aged woman go into a full run as she charged down my little hallway.

"Mr. Selby!" came the voice.

I stood up as she proceeded to give me a giant hug. My hair had turned gray and I'd added a few pounds. She, too, had aged. Rosa was no longer the adolescent girl I had known at Lincoln, but was a middle-aged mother with a daughter who was having problems. Rosa explained that another girl, a Mayra G., who was several years older than her daughter, wanted to fight her. Originally the two of them had been friends, but this was one of those high school friendships that had gone awry. The problems between them had exacerbated, getting to the point where students throughout the school were involved and taking sides. Some were on Monica's side and others were on Mayra's side, and both had many friends. The stage was set for a major conflict.

While I listened to Rosa I knew what she was describing was not the type of situation that I as a school psychologist should be handling. In this case we were talking about major conflict and possible gang issues. Monica needed to be referred to one of the deans, or perhaps even the school police. I had seen this type of thing before and knew that student unrest could lead to trouble, the kind that could escalate in this inner-city environment. I listened, knowing that I would have to tell Rosa I would not be dealing with her daughter and this other girl, but before I had a chance tears came to Rosa's eyes. She looked at me with a confidence that had developed some twenty years earlier. She dried her eyes with Kleenex.

"You can handle this," she said.

But I knew the truth. This was not a case that I would be taking on. I dealt with emotional issues and individual types of student problems. I talked with students in groups. It was not my job to be dealing with possible riots.

But Rosa was persuasive: "It looks like history repeats itself. You did it for me and now you can do it for my daughter."

Whoa! What is she talking about? I can't let her think that I'm going to handle this. I've got to stop this right now!

"Mr. Selby, you're my hero. You saved my life back then and I will never forget it. You're wonderful. You did it for me and now you can do it for my daughter."

She smiled: "You're my hero."

So that's the way it is. I'm her hero. Of course I can handle this.

And without me realizing it another of my most interesting experiences was on the way.

"I will call you later today and let you know how it goes."

Rosa exited the office and as she did so I immediately went into action. I wrote out two summons slips and went to the attendance office where I found a service worker: "Take this one out first and five minutes later get the second one."

I scheduled Monica to be the first of the two to come to my office. Several minutes later she entered and from the way she looked it was clear that something was bothering her. She told me that problems had escalated between her and Mayra. She had been hearing words of support from some of the Garfield students, while there had been threats from others. Her description about how the various students were reacting confirmed my suspicions: a fight and possible riot were about to happen.

Monica explained: There was a boy who she was not interested in, but he was interested in her. And not only was he interested, he had made a series of advances, except there was one minor problem. This boy already had a girlfriend and it was Mayra, the girl who now wanted to fight her.

My stomach reacted and I couldn't believe what she was telling to me. This was exactly the same type of situation that her mother had faced some twenty years earlier, except in her mother's case there were three girls instead of one.

Monica had just completed explaining the situation when down the hallway came Mayra. Unlike the characteristic *chola* (gangster) dress of Rosa's day, with the belt pulled in tightly at the waist and with well-ironed and creased pants, and with a flannel shirt concealing the bust line, Mayra wore jeans and they were skintight. Her blouse was form-fitting and the top two buttons were unfastened. The remaining buttons burst at the seams. Mascara, the one ingredient that united the two generations, was heavy.

"You want to see me?" Mayra stated abruptly. Her eyes caught sight of Monica. "I don't want to be here with that bitch. With that 'ho." (The shortened version for whore.) Hood rat was another of the more commonly used insults.

Monica sat in the corner, not responding.

"We're here to talk. We're here to see if we can get this situation calmed down." Mayra remained close to the door. If she wanted to make a quick exit, she was in a position where she would have a clear getaway. "We're just going to talk."

Mayra turned to check out this room. Her path to safety was still secure. Was there anyone else who was entering the room? No, there was not. Her eyes returned to me. Who was I? Momentarily she was confused. What was going on? And here in front of her was her enemy. It was then, and out of a natural kind of reflex response, she made a feint towards Monica. Neither Monica nor I responded, but we were aware. Suddenly she turned to leave and I thought the conference had just ended. Sometimes conferences do end just that quickly. She started down the little hallway, but decided she wasn't done. She wasn't going to just walk away when the enemy was there. She came back.

"You're just a bitch, a tramp, a hood rat." She gave Monica the evil eye. "You've been asking for it and now you're going to get it. Bitch! 'Ho."

Every ten seconds or so she turned to assure herself that this office wasn't a trap.

"We're just going to talk," I repeated. "It's just going to be us."

"I don't want to be here. I don't want to be here with this bitch, this hood rat."

Anger poured out of every cell. Her movements were uneven and mechanical; she paced back and forth. I watched and was ready, if it were necessary, to intervene, and I knew I was taking a chance by trying to handle this by myself. Other adults have been injured as they placed themselves in these types of situations. A friend, an assistant principal, had received a black eye when one of the girls he was working with hit him.

I kept careful watch on Mayra and like a lioness she stalked her prey. Around my office she moved, eyeing her enemy. She swaggered and thrust out her chest. She was sending a message not just of dominance, but she was letting this ninth grader know that here was the real deal. How dare this skinny, underdeveloped girl try to steal her man?

"I don't want to be here with that slut."

But it is at this point that an important issue needs to be clarified. It takes two people to fight and Monica was not cooperating. Mayra came within five feet of the stationary Monica and thrust out her chest. She continually gave the evil eye, something that is taken very seriously in the Latino culture. She stood directly in front of her. How could Monica think that she could compete against this?

It was time for me to get started.

"We're here to talk." I looked directly at Mayra. "I'm not an administrator. I'm not school police. I'm not a dean. I'm the school psychologist."

I wanted her to think about what I was saying, and I wanted to create an atmosphere where she might be willing to do something that she hadn't done before, and that was to listen to this foe of hers.

"I bring students in here to talk. I do this all the time."

She eyed her enemy: "You've been talking trash about me. You've been spreading all of these lies. You've been calling me a bitch. People say you've been calling me a lot of things. And we're ready. You're a 'ho. We're ready."

Monica still did not move, purposely avoiding eye contact, but the moment had come for her to show what she was made of. She had come into this office with a purpose and if any of these concerns were to be resolved, she knew she had to take an active role. Her head came up and she looked into the eyes of her aggressor.

"I haven't been calling you any names."

Transformation! Where before there was weakness and avoidance, now she had come out of her shell. There was strength and what I was observing reminded me of a similar student some twenty years earlier. I watched. Genetics had kicked in.

"I haven't called you any names and I haven't had anything to do with this." It was time to fight back. "Everyone has become involved in this. They want to see us fight. I don't want to fight you and this has nothing to do with us."

Monica's eyes pierced that previously impenetrable armor and Mayra stepped back.

"I think this is because of Juan. I think he's the one who wants this whole thing to get started and I think he's causing it."

"What's Juan got to do with this? We broke up. He has nothing to do with this."

"He does too! He asked me to go with him when he was going with you. He asked me several times and that was before the two of you broke up. I refused to go with him and I told him it wasn't right. He's hated me ever since. I also told him I was going to tell you, but I never did. The two of you broke up and I didn't think it was necessary. But he's still trying to get back at me and he's trying to get back at you. It's Juan who wants us to fight. I haven't said anything to others about you. It's Juan. He's the one who's causing the problem and by doing this he can back at both of us."

Communication, that important ingredient that can bring truth to an uncomfortable situation, was occurring, but change in one's cognitive processing and intent doesn't occur immediately. It takes time for a locomotive to slow down and come to a stop and Mayra's locomotive was still steaming ahead.

"It's over more than just him. You've been talking trash about me. You've been saying all of these things."

"I have not! I haven't been saying anything. Juan comes to me and says things and he goes back to you. He says different things to you than what I've said, and because of him now everyone is taking sides. They want to see us fight. They want to become involved. I've never been interested in Juan."

They were discussing the issues and with this discussion the entire emotional tone changed.

"I never trusted him," Mayra responded. "He was a bastard."

With the two of them now focusing in on what the real issues were, I was aware that there were other girls who had also complained about Juan's inappropriate advances. He was one of those individuals who tried "to come on" to many of the Garfield girls.

"He was always lying when we were together. He was always trying to find someone else. He thought he was so smooth, that he could get away with anything. He had me, but he wanted others.

He thought he was such a player. We broke up when I told him I didn't want to deal with his lies. I thought I was in love with him but he just played me. That's why we broke up."

It takes two to have communication and it takes a realistic appraisal of the issues from both sides, and they were accomplishing all of this without anger or threats. They had reached a point where they were both ready to look and understand what was happening. I sat down and became the observer.

Twenty minutes later: "Everything's okay between us," Mayra said. "We're not going to fight."

Monica agreed and the bell rang.

"Can we go to lunch?" they asked.

"Sure."

They walked out the door together. I took a deep breath and went to my window. I could breathe much easier now as I looked at the panorama of the surrounding neighborhood, the houses, and to the grassy area three stories below. The weather was heating up and my office would soon be feeling its effects. I thought about Monica's mother and what had happened some twenty years earlier. I would never forget that experience or the one that had just happened. *Thank God it's over*, I thought to myself, *and that it went well. I'm so glad that it went well and that I didn't have to physically intervene! I'm glad I didn't get a black eye.*

I turned from the window, realizing there was one last thing for me to do. Rosa was anxiously awaiting my call. I picked up the phone and dialed her number: "Everything is okay. Its all been settled and they're not going to fight. In fact they're once again friends. The whole thing was a misunderstanding. It all started because of a boy."

"A boy? A boy? That's what happened to me. Don't you remember Mr. Selby? My problem started because a boy walked me to class. Don't you remember?"

"Yes, Rosa, I remember."

"Mr. Selby..."

"Yes, Rosa."

"You're still my hero."

"Thanks, Rosa."

This incident happened when Monica was a ninth grader. She continued to do very well in school that year and had no more difficulties. The following year she no longer needed the support from the Focus group and I rarely saw her. Everything was going well. But it was during Monica's junior year that Rosa decided it was time to take Monica back to the Lincoln High School. Lincoln, of course, was where Rosa had graduated and where she continued to have many close friends. To Rosa, Lincoln High School was home. Lincoln High School and the surrounding community was where her daughter needed to be.

Approximately two years later Rosa called and told me that Monica had graduated and that she was soon to marry. I have not heard from either of them since that time, but their experiences will live with me forever.

CHAPTER 12

THE GIRL WITH THE FROGGY VOICE

PART ONE

In recent years, special education has come to the forefront because of the many new laws and regulations that schools are required to meet. Instead of students with severe physical or mental disabilities being placed in a special education school, which was the way it was previously done, now whenever possible these students are placed in the regular public school environment. Individual aides are provided to these students when it is necessary. This story, however, begins when the district was going through some of those early growing pains in regard to the types of services offered through special education and how best to meet needs of these students.

It was 1995 and Garfield was off to its typical start. We had students without classes, teachers without students, teachers with fifty students and, within this entire mix, there were the counselors who were doing the best they could to make adjustments. After several weeks it all calmed down.

In mid-October I received a phone call. The office of special education contacted me concerning a new class that we had just put into operation. It was known as Community Based Instruction (CBI) and it was designed to deal with our most special of students, the retarded students. Previously these students had been placed in a class called "ER", standing for educably retarded. Now, however, in the CBI classroom these students with the more severe of learning difficulties had been placed into a different learning environment. In their previous setting the emphasis was on reading, writing and arithmetic, but now the emphasis was placed on life and basic survival skills. The goal of this class was to have these students eventually placed in jobs.

One morning I received a phone call: "We really like your CBI classroom."

This was one of those early morning wakeup calls from a specialist at the district offices.

"We think your teachers are doing a very good job."

"I'm really proud of them, too."

Though the class had only been instituted several weeks earlier, the two teachers had taken this new task to heart and were doing an excellent job, in spite of the difficulties related to learning an entirely new curriculum. The two of them were accomplishing this in a team-teaching atmosphere with their two classes combined.

"We think your class is so good, in fact," came her next statement, "that we are assigning another student to it. She'll be arriving in a couple of days. She's has a few more problems than your other students, but don't worry. The committee felt she would do just fine at your school."

Bingo! I knew what was going on. The area office had already made the determination and not one person from our school had been involved in the decision making process; they had done this type of thing too many times in the past. I felt a lump deep within my stomach.

"Your program appears to be the best."

More of the standard jargon.

"We're still waiting for transportation to be arranged. Mother will be giving you a call later today."

Then came the dial tone. But from an innocent and unsuspecting beginning was set in motion behaviors and emotions which none of us at Garfield had ever before seen. However, before describing what followed as a result of this phone call, it is first necessary to take a closer look at that highly praised Community Based Instruction classroom. The classroom consisted of two teachers team-teaching in one room, but they were teaching the equivalent of two standard-sized special education classes.

In this one classroom, which was of average size and that had been previously used for just one of our special education classes, were squeezed twenty-six mentally retarded students, two teachers and two teaching assistants. The students were already packed to the rafters, knocking heads with each other, and with this additional student it was only going to get worse.

But there was another and more immediate concern. What did this specialist mean when she said, "This student has a few more problems than your other students, but don't worry. The committee felt you could handle it." What kinds of problems was this specialist referring to, and how did some committee that didn't have even one representative from Garfield know what we could and could not handle? I glanced out the window and noticed in the early morning haze a dark cloud was hovering directly above Garfield High School. It centered itself over our struggling CBI classroom. Realizing that these two teachers needed to be informed as soon as possible, I set out for the CBI classroom, room 802.

Several minutes later I arrived. The door was closed. Did I want to go in? I did not, but I knew they needed to be informed and this was my job. I entered. Many students were already in the process of going on an excursion to the Laundromat where they were learning to do the laundry. A line was forming at the furthest door. After about thirty seconds, the two teachers, David Foster and Vivian Zamorano, came over and from their facial expressions I could see that they were both feeling the strain of the constant activities required of them each day.

"Guess what?" I began. "I just had a call from the district offices. We're getting a new student." I had decided to give them this information without going slowly. I felt it would be best to simply get straight to the point.

"You're crazy," Vivian shot back. Maybe I should have slowed down and gradually built into it?

Vivian is about five feet tall and weighs approximately 100 pounds. She'd never been known to keep her opinions to herself on educational issues that she considered to be important. And this was definitely one of those issues. Yes, she was upset.

"What are we going to do?" she immediately asked. "What are we supposed to do?"

Her frustration was obvious. The experienced and usually taciturn David Foster stood without making a move. Finally, when he'd had the time to think about it, he responded: "We don't have any more room. We don't have any more chairs." His arms reached skyward, demonstrating what might have been interpreted as some kind of a prayer to an all caring and loving God, but there was no heavenly response. So out of his frustration he emphasized his point one more time: "We don't have any place to put someone," finishing with, "We don't have any chairs. This is crazy!"

"You're right!" I agreed with him and with Vivian. But this was not something that any of us had a choice in.

"Well," Dave Foster continued, "I'm going back to my government job!"

This was the surest sign that he'd been pushed beyond his limit. We could hear the students in their excitement were ready to leave. Two lines had formed and the destination of the Laundromat held a wealth of hidden possibilities.

"The specialist called me just fifteen minutes ago. This girl will be here in a couple of days and there's nothing that can be done. The only thing remaining is to arrange transportation. Once this is done, and it's not going to take long, she's going to become our student."

That's the way it began. I did what I had to do and had delivered the message. Later, just as had been indicated, I received a phone call: "Hello, is this the school psychologist?"

"Yes, it is."

"This is Mrs. G. My daughter will be enrolling at Garfield in the next couple of days and will enter the CBI class. I'd like to come to the school and discuss some special concerns with you about her."

We set the meeting for the following morning at nine o'clock.

CHAPTER 13

THE GIRL WITH THE FROGGY VOICE

PART TWO

Our new student was Brenda, but why was she being sent to Garfield High School? Prior to enrolling at our school, I later learned that her class was for students that had more than one handicapping condition. I knew I would soon be talking with mother and getting additional information, but the most important question would have to wait for an answer: would she be able to fit into our much larger school?

It was nine o'clock when Mrs. G. arrived. She was approximately thirty-five years old and she dressed professionally. I remember that I was immediately impressed, but I also knew that we had important business to discuss. I invited her to sit down, but when we were ready to begin she started, but suddenly stopped herself. She moved back and forth uncomfortably in her chair.

"How can I help?" I asked.

Her eyes turned to me. "I'm not sure." She crossed one leg, uncrossed it, and then crossed it in the other direction. "I talked with the people at the previous meeting (the special education meeting where this placement had been made) and they said it was important for me to come in and talk with you before Brenda begins. They said there were a lot of things I would need to discuss and I knew it was true. It's just hard for me to do this. There's always so much that I have to explain. Brenda is very different from the other children and she always has been. She's very loving and caring. She's been tested and has an I.Q. of fifty-two."

I.Q. scores were no longer used in the Los Angeles Unified School District, but, nevertheless, this was important information. This score placed her within the range of moderate mental retardation. Most of the students within this CBI classroom functioned within the mild range of mental retardation, which was somewhat higher, but there were a few students also within this lower range. However, I was about to learn there was more involved than just her intellectual functioning.

"Brenda has been classified as both schizophrenic and autistic. She's been to many doctors. I think the doctors themselves are confused on how to classify her or what her problems are. I want you to know that she has a friend she talks to. This is an imaginary friend. She will also talk about having two babies and she talks about them quite often. They are imaginary. When she is nervous she is especially likely to talk about them. I'm sure that she'll discuss them when you meet her. Brenda is a very loving and trusting child. If someone told her to take her clothes off, she would do it. She did well in her other school, but it was much smaller. Brenda is so excited about coming here. She has seen the movie "Stand and Deliver" about Jaime Escalante and your math students at least two hundred times. All she does is talk about Garfield."

"How large was the school she is coming from?"

"It had eight hundred students."

"How large was the class she was in?"

"There were eight students. There was one teacher and four aides."

Garfield was more than five times the size of her previous school. Brenda was also coming from what was classified as the most special of special education classes, a classroom that handled multiple handicaps. In this setting all of students were dealing with more than one handicapping condition. In our CBI classroom we would not be able to provide the same level of support she had previously received.

I explained, "We have two teachers and two aides in the one classroom. There are currently twenty-four students and it's very crowded. These students eat in the cafeteria with the other students. During nutrition and lunch, they are treated like everyone else and they receive the same supervision as everyone else within the school."

The Los Angeles Unified School District was soon to be sued for not complying with mandated special education requirements. Brenda was enrolling before this lawsuit took place. If she had enrolled two years later when it was more common for students to be assigned an individual aide, her adjustment would have been much more controlled and any difficulties could more effectively be handled.

Mother began to cry; I gave her the box of Kleenex. We both knew Garfield would be a challenge for Brenda and that her success at Garfield was not guaranteed.

"We'll do everything we can to make it successful." I waited until she wiped her eyes. "We want it to be successful, but if something happens where it looks like it isn't going to work, or if at any time we need to talk about a problem, I'll immediately give you a call. I also want you to know that we're a very good school and the class she's entering is considered to be one the finest in this section of the city."

It hadn't been our decision for Brenda to be a part of our program, but we would do everything possible to ensure her success. Both David Foster and Vivian Zamorano wanted all of their students to do well. They were both teachers who were loving, kind and protective. Once Brenda started this class she would be under their protective umbrella. In their minds these students were like their own children.

And me? What was to be my role after this initial conference with mother? Well, I had become the go-between and it was to be my responsibility to ensure that Brenda's transition be done as effectively as possible. We arranged that when Brenda and her mother came into school the following day she would be introduced to some of the Garfield staff: the deans, her counselor, the special education class, and anyone else who might be involved. Mother would bring her to my office where we would first talk and then we would set out to the school and meet some of the important people.

It was nine when mother and daughter arrived. I was seated at my small table. I heard noise and Brenda rushed in.

"I'm so excited," she screamed.

Mother lagged several steps behind.

"Counselor," Brenda continued, "I'm so excited! I'm coming to Garfield High School. Counselor, I'm so excited."

Following this, she bounced and skipped around the office, moving from one side to the other. She wore a white chiffon dress with black shoes and dark black socks. She was of average height and build, with skin the color of pearls. She smiled as she spun and her white teeth glistened.

"I'm so excited, counselor. I'm so excited."

I didn't know what to say so I just watched. I had never before had a student who was excited about coming to Garfield.

"Garfield is the best school in the world. I'm so excited counselor. It's the best school in the world. I love Garfield High School," and with this announcement she suddenly charged out of the office. Mother and I quickly got up from out chairs and followed, only to see her going down the stairwell to the right. We raced after her.

Down the stairs she went and she turned to her left on the second floor. There were several offices on this floor, but it was to be the deans' office where she made her first appearance.

The deans' office is where justice is meted out for all of those students who have been unable to successfully comply with the school's rules. Our first adventure was on its way.

Mother and I entered the deans' office only to see the benches overflowing with students. Here were the boys who could do no right and the girls who could do no wrong. Shoulder to shoulder they sat while five to ten additional students stood near the open door. It was early, but this was clearly a busy day, and in the middle was Brenda. She had taken a position on center stage, directly in the middle of the large room and all eyes were upon her. She stood very still, looking back at them.

A secretary stationed to the side, whose job it was to keep order, yelled: "I hear some talking. No one talks when they come in here."

Mother quickly yanked Brenda to the side while I quietly motioned for them to wait. I went to get the two deans, Jan Torres and Paul Purdy, whose two offices were to the rear. I stood between their two open doors and got their attention. But each was under the belief that what they were doing had precedent. "It's an emergency," I repeated and I stood my ground. They didn't want to, but they came with me. We went to the larger waiting area and I made some introductions: "Ms. Torres and Mr. Purdy," I began, "this is the new student I was talking with you about yesterday. Her name is Brenda and this is Mrs. G., Brenda's mother."

Mr. Purdy began: "And Brenda, we're happy to have you with us. Let us know if you have any problems."

It was now Brenda's turn: "I love Garfield High School." She spoke in a loud voice and followed that up with: "I'm so excited. I love Garfield High School," and she began running through this crowed room, jumping up and down and occasionally doing a twirl. The office became unusually quiet. Brenda clapped her hands and continued twirling, finishing this up with, "I love Garfield. I love this place. I'm so happy to be here."

Well, Mr. Purdy had seen enough: "Brenda, we're happy to have you, too. Perhaps you should move on to your next appointment."

Yes, it was time to be moving on and after this one stop there would be no more visits to the other offices. The deans' office and this one adventure had been sufficient. The CBI classroom would be our next destination. Success or failure, after all, would be determined by how she adjusted to this new classroom and to the larger school environment.

From the deans' office, it was an easy walk and it was only supposed to take two minutes. But once we got down the stairs something happened. Brenda's head thrust downward and each step became more difficult than the last. Her smile, which had been one of her distinctive characteristics, disappeared and in its place was a grimace. Our progress was very slow and we had to take great care to prevent her from crashing into the walls.

What happened? I thought. *One minute she was twirling in ecstasy and the next she needs the two of us to guide her and to keep her from running into trashcans.*

Like Dr. Jeckle and Mr. Hyde, Brenda had gone through a strange metamorphosis. From the happy and bubbly personality who'd entertained us earlier, she'd become a lethargic shadow of herself. She came to a complete stop and her arms fell downward like useless clay appendages. We were somewhere between the deans' office and her new classroom and she turned and faced an empty wall.

"Brenda," I asked, "what's wrong?" I moved close and then it came, a deep guttural sound, like a frog.

"I'm afraid, counselor."

She was speaking in a froggy voice. I took a step back and turned to mother.

"Nothing to worry about," mom responded. "Brenda does this sometimes when she gets worried. She's been receiving speech therapy to correct this pattern."

So much for speech therapy. What followed remains somewhat unclear, though we started moving. Mostly I remember that my conversation focused primarily upon whether or not Pinocchio was a real boy or if Dumbo could fly? We turned one corner and the next and the next. Step by step we made our way to this new environment. Several minutes later we stood at the stairs leading into the class. Sounds could be heard coming from within.

"Oh counselor," came the guttural mutterings of this Pee Wee Herman facsimile. The words came out very, very slowly. "I hope they like me. I'm really nervous. What if they don't like me?"

Good question! What if they don't like her? What if she doesn't fit in? What would we do then? I held the door open and mother entered, followed by Brenda. The students were in their seats awaiting the new arrival. I closed the door while twenty-four sets of eyes focused in our direction. The students were quiet, excited, and watchful. The teachers, Zamorano and Foster, came over, as did one of the two classroom aides. Calmly, and trying not to create unnecessary excitement which might be perceived by Brenda as threatening, I introduced her to the class.

"This is Brenda and she's going to be coming into the class. She'll be joining us in a couple of days."

You could feel the sizzle within the classroom as the three of us stood there. Brenda, unfortunately, didn't share this excitement. She stood frozen like a Popsicle, with head down, body stiff and arms clinging tenaciously to her sides. The students watched and waited, while the two teachers, mother and I carried on a quiet conversation. Gradually, however, Brenda's head inched upward and she took a glance around the room. Her head suddenly shot downward, but after about twenty seconds she did it again. It wasn't too obvious, but by doing it this way she could see that here in this isolated classroom was a different world. Here were her compatriots, fellow students sheltered from the pressures and threats from the outside environment. Her chin raised an inch and then her head came up to stay. Seven rows of students faced her, patiently waiting for this new addition. Four or five of the girls watched closely.

In this world for the retarded and the severely disabled, Brenda was viewed as a potential friend, an ally and as part of an important support system. Alone on this campus and in the external world these students felt vulnerable and afraid, but together they could effectively navigate the currents and undercurrents of whatever might happen to them and together they could survive. One of these girls rose from her seat and approached Brenda.

Brenda announced: "I have two babies. I'm going to tell them that I'm at Garfield High School."

Another student, a girl seated in the furthermost corner, got up from her seat.

"You have two babies. I have a baby," producing a picture of herself and her new born child. The baby was approximately two months old.

The ice had been broken and the necessary adjustments were taking place. This girl with the baby picture put it back into her purse and returned to her seat. We didn't tell Brenda or her mother, but this two month-old child had been temporarily taken away from her retarded mother. In an angry moment this student had accidentally broken the child's leg and she didn't understand what she'd done that was wrong. A court case was pending to determine whether or not this girl was an appropriate mother and could properly care for this child. The infant was later returned. Unfortunately, this student again became pregnant a second time. After the birth of this second child, she no longer attended school.

As the three of us left the class we were all feeling quite good about the basic introduction. We knew that we had accomplished what we needed to accomplish. Now all that remained was transportation and this was scheduled to begin in two days.

It became my responsibility to meet her at the bus on this first day and ensure that there weren't any mishaps.

CHAPTER 14

THE GIRL WITH THE FROGGY VOICE

PART THREE

Two days later and some forty-five minutes before the morning bell I made some visits. I checked with the attendance office to remind them that our new student was arriving and I also talked with Brenda's grade counselor. I'd decided to make a quick stop at the deans' office. Our two deans did not need any reminding.

"Prancer is coming today," Purdy announced. "I can hardly wait."

Ms. Torres: "Prancer, you mean Dancer. We can all learn a few steps."

So much for the two of them. I had other concerns on my mind. I went to room 802. The door was open and Foster and Zamorano were waiting and wondering: What were they going to do with Brenda and how was she going to fit in? How were they going to be receptive to her individual needs, and what would be these individual needs? This was how it went:

"I don't know about this Selby," began Zamorano. "I just don't know."

"I don't know about this either Zamorano."

Standing by Zamorano was Dave Foster. His full beard stretched from ear to ear and he was motionless, except for the faint sound of his breathing. His respiration stopped and his eyes starred into space. Finally, "Selby… Selby…what are we doing?"

Foster was right. What were we doing?

"You know if this doesn't work out, I'm going back to my government job."

Dave was reminiscing of a time when he didn't have to deal with the school district and the way it too frequently made decisions. Unable to answer their questions or to provide any additional information or support, it was time for me to be moving on.

Twenty minutes later I'd placed myself next to Officer Crosby, our school policeman, in front of the school. He was a truly nice guy and by far the finest school policeman we'd ever had. He was firm, but he had compassion. The two of us stood together, eyes focused on the street. Parents dropped off their children. Officer Crosby's presence was letting everyone know that when he was there this school was safe. Several minutes later a tiny yellow bus turned the corner and pulled next to the curb and stopped. Finally the door swung open and out came two of the CBI students, followed by Brenda.

My eyes were glued upon her as I watched, like an eagle concentrating on its prey. Yes, Brenda had arrived and she was with a group of our CBI students. She began walking toward the school when suddenly she broke into a charge, down the grass and up the stairs. With head down and full speed forward, she barreled towards the two of us. Officer Crosby had stationed himself on one side of the large external doors while I was at the other. Then, and with no words or eye contact, and adroitly avoiding collisions with other students, up the stairs she flew, through the open doors, down the hall she sped, and she disappeared.

Officer Crosby, not one normally puzzled by the ebb and flow of the morning traffic, was a little taken back.

"What was that?" he said.

"A new student."

"Oh."

Three minutes later we both turned and went our individual ways. This was Brenda's first day and she had arrived safely to class. There were no incidents of any sort and with this beginning I could relax. I had done my job. I checked with the teachers as the day progressed and her adjustment appeared to be good. Foster, using the best of his ingenuity, had even secured an additional chair so that she could have a place to sit in class. He never told me how or where he got it. Before we knew it a week had gone by.

The days turned into weeks and the weeks into months, and as we dealt with her we learned that she was like none of our other students. It was impossible to determine how she might act or what she might say from one moment to the next. Would she be talking to her babies, speaking in a deep voice, hiding, or excited? She could be withdrawn or effervescent, or perhaps she might be performing one of her dances, and you never knew where that might happen. There was one student, Jeannie, who took it upon herself to discuss Brenda with me one morning: "I think Brenda is crazy. Babies, I don't think she has any babies. I think she is so funny. I think she is crazy." Jeannie laughed and soon it was all forgotten.

The weeks flowed by and soon two months had passed. Zamorano and Foster beamed, and for them the truth was self-evident. They really were two of the best teachers in the district, miracle workers to say the least, while success followed upon success. Life was good, not only for them but for the entire school. Our football team was winning, and in high school there is nothing more important than having a winning football team. And not only that, in accompaniment of our winning ways in football we had a championship drill team. Garfield was the best that high school had to offer.

But somehow or another, perhaps because of our many successes, and perhaps it was because at this large school we were constantly dealing with so many crises, we had forgotten about Brenda and those debilitating issues with which she lived. Sadly, we'd forgotten about the realities of our environment. Garfield, located in East Los Angeles, was an inner-city school and Brenda, in spite of an apparent smooth transition, was different from all of our other students. She made no friends. Even in her special education class where everyone banned together in order to survive, either because of her autism or schizophrenia, she lacked that internal capacity to relate to others. She was a loner.

Now, as I write about this many, many years later, her differences and handicapping conditions seem so obvious, but after those first tranquil weeks we forgot. Even Officer Crosby, our unemotional steward of authority and law and order, was lulled into a state of complacency when Brenda came up to him and said, "Policeman, I love this school." She did her little pirouette, skipped and pranced. Officer Crosby would look at her and, while trying to maintain a semblance of the authoritarian image, would say, "I know you do, Brenda. I know you do." And sometimes he would tell her, "Brenda, if anyone bothers you, you let me know." She would look at him and smile and scamper off to another part of the campus.

All was quiet and serene on the outside. While the adults were sympathetic and understanding, many of our students were beginning to wonder about the behavior of this strange interloper who made it a habit of charging into conversations and acting inappropriately. Her actions were drawing attention. Skipping along on a serpentine path, jumping, dancing and usually talking to herself, she was alone among more than four thousand students. Innocent and kind, and incapable of defending herself, she was a lamb amongst wolves; and we were soon to learn there were many wolves. And if there was a problem she was incapable of telling anyone.

One day just as fourth period was coming to a close and as I was preparing to go to the teachers' cafeteria, Ms. Daniels, the assistant principal in charge of the attendance office, approached.

"I think Brenda was having some problems at nutrition. Can you look into it?"

"What happened?"

"Oh, I don't think it was anything too serious. I think some kids were taunting her. Can you look into it?"

Ms. Daniels shrugged her shoulders in a questioning manner and left me to decide how important this was, and to determine an appropriate course of action. But as a result I was somewhat confused. Was there a problem? And if there was a problem was it necessary for me to look into it? She walked away, but after about ten feet she turned, "Let me know if there is a problem."

Whether or not there was a problem, it had now become my responsibility to make some sort of a determination. Unfortunately, when the assistant principal spoke to me lunch was about to begin and I was already making my way to the cafeteria. My immediate goal was to get to the teachers' cafeteria and the all-important microwave. Thirty seconds delay here could mean ten minutes of waiting in line. So it was off to the cafeteria I went, immediately forgetting about whatever it was that Ms. Daniels wanted me to look into.

Two minutes later I had my food warmed and I sat comfortably in my chair. My buddies arrived. We ate. We joked and I was having a wonderfully good time. Yes, I was enjoying myself, feeling relaxed, until suddenly Ms. Daniels' words came back: "I think some kids were taunting Brenda. Can you look into it?" Yes, I really did need to look into this. I began picking up what I had remaining on my tray, preparing to leave.

"What are you doing?" Walt Atwood asked. "Man we're just getting started." He gave me one of his surprised looks as several others now joined us at the table.

"Got to go."

"We can see that," and again he gave me his look.

I left the table and was about to exit through the rear section of the cafeteria when something did not seem right and a cold shiver ran up my spine. Was it my imagination, but were strange sounds emanating from outside the exterior door? I heard a loud shriek. I rushed through the door and directly to my right was Brenda, standing alone. Retarded, schizophrenic, or possibly autistic, she was unable to cope with the external threat that she was experiencing. Instead of leaving the area and going to safety, as most students would have done, she reacted like a wild animal. Her body bent backwards and strange yells and howls reached skywards.

I approached: "Come on Brenda, let's go."

She didn't recognize me. Hysterical screams shot upward and her arms thrust mechanically into the air. Her spine curved backwards. She was lost. Brenda had entered a world that she alone knew and where existence was separate and distinct from the realities around her.

Then I heard: "Crazy! Stupid! *Estupida!* Crazy! *Loca!*"

Words and taunts sprang from a group of students some thirty yards away. Words that to the normal student would cause uneasiness and anxiety and words that would lead a normal student to find safety. But to the unstable mind of Brenda these were the triggers that sent her deep within.

"*Puta!* (Whore) Crazy! Loca! Crazy!"

More words and, as they came, she withdrew to the recesses of her primitive mind. An apple careened by the two of us. Her screams filled the surroundings. She was fighting demons, but she didn't know what they were or where they came from. Unable to run, unable to hide, and unable to determine the cause of this inner turmoil, she retreated to a place that only she knew. Another apple was thrown. I left Brenda and went toward these students only so see them disappear. I returned to find a student unaware of me or of the world around her.

Several minutes later the bell sounded and in a conditioned response she went to her class. She walked in with the rest of the students. She sat in her seat. It was here where she could again find safety and security. Tears formed and she cried. She talked to an imaginary friend and to her babies. Zamorano and Foster tried to communicate with her but she shut everyone out.

We didn't know it, but this was to be her last day at our school. Brenda was special, more special than any of us had thought, and though we liked her and wanted her to be successful, Garfield was inappropriate. Ms. Daniels was concerned for her safety and set up a meeting. Brenda was approved for special funding that would permit her to be placed in a private school reserved for those with the most severe of problems.

The placement for Brenda was supervised by a special office within the district. An administrator from this office would make recommendations of possible schools that seemed appropriate and send mother out to visit them. Normally this selection process takes no more than two weeks, but in Brenda's case it was to take three months. The special schools were reticent to accept a student with problems as severe as hers and we all knew that if she were to be successful she needed to be placed in a supportive and safe environment. And throughout these months Brenda waited at home.

It took time. I waited and wondered, and I must confess there was a point when I thought an appropriate school would never be found. But at last the day came when mother called. They had found a school in Orange County. "Brenda," mother stated, "says it's the best school in the world." I laughed. Yes, Brenda had found the best school in the world.

Brenda and her babies, and her imaginary friend and froggy voice, and her Dr. Jeckel and Mr. Hyde personality have now been gone for many years. All of her classmates have moved on and others have taken their places. The indelible mark this one girl left upon us has faded and become indistinct, but it has not completely disappeared. There are still a few people at the school who remember her.

But as is always the case, over time we've seen many changes. Ms. Zamorano, the expert in Community Based Instruction, decided to change schools. I retired. Several years after I retired, Dave Foster also retired and moved to Arizona.

It was in 2012 when Dave Foster and I finally had a chance to reminisce about some of our experiences. We were both older, but our sense of humor had remained.

"After you left," Foster stated, "there wasn't anyone like you. You really enjoyed our kids. You knew all of our students and they loved having you come in to talk with them."

"Your class was my favorite class." And I asked, "Do you remember Brenda?"

"Brenda?" and he thought for a minute. "Yes, how could I ever forget Brenda? She was the one with the froggy voice. She was the one with the imaginary friend and the fake babies. I never knew what Brenda was going to do. She was fun. I wonder what ever happened to her."

"She went off to Orange County and found a school that she loved. She said, 'It's the best school in the world.'"

"Well, I miss her. She was truly a very special student. More different than any of the others, but she was a lot of fun."

CHAPTER 15

BULLDOG RUSH

PART ONE

In 1995 our varsity football team, the mighty Bulldogs, was on its way to having one of its best seasons ever. Week after week they won, frequently outscoring their opponents by two, three, or even four touchdowns. Dominance, the name of the game in football, is what it's all about and this was a season that comes once in every twenty or thirty years. Our school in East Los Angeles was gaining headlines and the truth was out. We were invincible.

It was late in the season. The final game was almost upon us and it was against our cross-town rivals, Roosevelt High School. Though this game was still several weeks away, the tension against those Rough Riders was building. Garfield had a tradition that before this game the varsity players would run through the halls and, in united camaraderie, yell and scream. It was "shish-boom-bah, win-win-win," and all that never-to-be-forgotten high school spirit that makes for an unforgettable high school experience.

But this season was not like previous years. Approximately ten days prior to the game all was not going well for Garfield's varsity. Teachers at the monthly faculty meeting questioned the value of Bulldog Rush. To these teachers this activity was placing the emphasis at Garfield in the wrong areas. "Education" they emphasized, "is important, not football games." But their concerns dealt with much more than just education. "Let's not forget about something called sportsmanship," these teachers complained. Though these players were winning, sportsmanship was a commodity that was in short supply. Questions were raised: Were we dealing with student-athletes who didn't care about anyone but themselves? Were they a group of individuals who somehow hadn't internalized basic human values? These were good questions and the longer this meeting lasted the more the complaints escalated.

A history teacher stated it like this: "Many of the players don't appear to have respect for anyone or anything."

An English teacher asked: "What are we promoting, education or hooliganism?"

A female teacher added: "Sexual slurs are constant with these players. They continually put women down and they don't care who hears. They have no respect for the opposite sex. I can't believe the complaints I've heard from many girls. This is wrong and we have to do something!"

This meeting brought out the emotions of the teachers. What could be done to emphasize to the players that their behavior off the football field needed to change? A vote was taken: "All those who no longer want these players running through the halls prior to the big game, raise your hands." It was almost unanimous. There would be no more Bulldog Rush and the faculty had spoken. The school's administration was in agreement. These football machos had ruled long enough and it was time for them to have a better and more realistic perspective of what life was all about.

The following week and just two days before the Friday night game everything was normal. Sixth period was coming to a close and some students had already turned in their final assignments while others had begun placing various materials in their backpacks.

The weather on that November day was warm. The Santa Ana breezes that visit Southern California from time to time had once again blanketed the region with dry warm weather. The birds in one of the school's exterior trees were the first to take notice. Their chirping came to a halt, and within thirty seconds faint but perceptible vibrations could be felt throughout the central buildings.

Yelling and noisemaking was the ostensible purpose. Exciting the student body and instilling enthusiasm for the upcoming game was the intent. But these players had their own agenda. They were angry and the time had come for payback. The first indication that this wasn't going to be Bulldog Rush as normal was that two trash cans were toppled. Trash spewed down the hall. Then a window was broken. Fifty players dressed in tennis shoes, shorts, jerseys, and football helmets swarmed.

Mr. Matsushita, a biology teacher and an ex-football coach, recognized the familiar sounds of the approaching team. He was surprised, but he was one of those dissenting teachers who'd supported football and Bulldog Rush. He knew how valuable the entire football experience could be.

"Look, class," he told his students when he heard the distant rumblings, "we're having Bulldog Rush."

The students, all of them limited English speakers, rose from their seats. What was this thing that their teacher was so excited about?

"The students got up from their seats to see the players running by, but they didn't run by. Instead, they charged into my class and flattened my students," Mr. Matsushita told me. His voice was soft and his manner somber. A tear came to his eye. Mr. Matsushita was tough, but he was also sensitive and caring. As he spoke I knew that he was very upset. "Many of these students were not just limited English speaking, but some were completely non-English speaking. They had no idea about what was going on. These players dressed in shorts, jerseys and helmets charged into them. It was students and desks flying everywhere."

During the melee that followed, it was said that Mr. Matsushita fly-tackled one of the most unruly of the group. Five feet-four inches tall and one hundred fifty pounds, he tackled a two hundred and forty pound football player. Other teachers and their classes experienced similar attacks, and several of our young female instructors had their physical safety threatened. Two of these female teachers were pushed against a wall as players taunted, yelled, pointed fingers and jumped skyward. One of our newest teachers was left in tears and it took time before she would fully recover.

CHAPTER 16

BULLDOG RUSH

PART TWO

The day after the team had completed its version of Bulldog Rush, disbelief among the teachers became widespread. The majority of the teachers were just becoming aware of what had happened the previous day because the players had not run through the sections of the school where their rooms were located.

The earliest information indicated that the players had organized their own version of Bulldog Rush, and not only had they run through the school when they weren't supposed to, but they had terrorized many of the classrooms in the 300, the 400, and the 600 buildings. These three buildings contained about twenty-five percent of the school's population. Teachers asked: Hadn't it been decided that this run would not be held? And hadn't the principal agreed with this request by the teachers?

This one event, perhaps more than anything else this school year, had an adverse affect on teacher morale. The disbelief on Thursday intensified by Friday. The time had come for the teachers to make a united statement to the principal and to the football players that this type of action would not be tolerated. The representative from the teachers' union became involved. All hell was about to break loose. What was going to be done to restore normalcy to the campus and to communicate teachers' concerns? There were also many teachers who felt that because of the players' actions the Friday night game should be cancelled. This may have been the way many felt, but this was not to happen. Garfield's varsity went on to an overwhelming victory.

The following Monday a hush fell over the morning cafeteria chatter. Carol Silva, a math teacher and one whose class had been invaded by the varsity players some five days earlier, sat unable to speak. And her husband Bill, who always had a smile and who only rarely complained, kept his head down. To the teachers at this table this was Garfield's "Darkest Monday."

At last Carol looked up: "What's going on here at this school?" The rest of us at the table remained silent. "They destroyed my class and physically threatened me. I've never been afraid of anything happening to me, until this happened."

Bill just shook his head: "And they still had the game! I don't believe it. They still had the game."

The bell rang for everyone to go to class, but no one moved. Bill was the first to get up: "I guess we have to go. It doesn't make any sense to me, but I have students waiting."

A lunchtime meeting had already been scheduled to discuss what had happened. Teachers were angry and this meeting was the first opportunity for teachers to get all of the facts and to make their concerns known. However, by the time many teachers arrived at the library, after purchasing their lunch, the bell rang to return to class. Tempers flared even more. In response to this, the principal scheduled another lunchtime meeting for the following day, extending the lunchtime period by fifteen minutes.

At the second meeting the library was filled to capacity. Most of the teachers who had their rooms invaded by the players were present. The varsity football coach was there as well as the union representative. As the facts were presented it continued to be somewhat unclear why this had happened. Neither the football coach nor the principal had authorized it. They were both unaware that it would happen. When this meeting concluded two themes seemed to predominate. The first conclusion of this meeting was that this action was not going to be easily forgotten or dismissed. The second conclusion was that additional time was needed to get clarify all of the concerns.

The principal and the union representative agreed that the next scheduled faculty meeting would be the best time for a full discussion, including all of the teachers, the principal and the coach. They decided that I, as the school psychologist, would act as the moderator.

This third and last meeting was held thirteen days after the players had run through the school. In order to start things off and set the overall tone, both the principal and the union representative spoke for approximately one minute. Then, as the school psychologist, it was my turn. I came to the podium and looked out at approximately one hundred and fifty teachers. All eyes were upon me. I explained what my task was, which was to give people a chance to get information about exactly what had happened and to voice their concerns. Did these teachers need any prompting? Hands were already raised.

I called upon one of our female teachers: "These players should all be lined up and have their balls cut off." But she wasn't done: "These players are all male-macho ass-holes who should have their balls cut off."

Some teachers applauded her while I could but wonder how the rest of the meeting would go. I acknowledged an English teacher. He had his Ph.D. in English and had published several books:

"That teacher is right, but the problem is football. It's an aggressive sport and teaches people to hurt and maim others. You can see how these players respond to the sport. We all know that not only on the football field but in the classroom these players are an insult to what we're trying to do here at Garfield High School."

More applause.

Next, and not far behind the "having the players' balls cut off" issue and "football is an aggressive sport that has no place on the high school campus" came a variety of teachers with the mind-set that all sports should be done away with. "We are educators," they said "and that's what we should be doing. Our academic scores are low. Get rid of all sports and place the emphasis where it needs to be placed, on reading, writing and arithmetic."

Teachers were angry and this was an opportunity to vent, to give their personal opinions about football and sports, and to discuss the various treatment options available. Eventually two decisions were reached. First and foremost was the unanimous opinion that these varsity football players needed to be punished. Their actions were compared to people outside of school who break the law. Society has a way of handling this and we, as a part of society, needed to do the same. These students were violators of the law and because of this they needed to be treated like the criminals they were. Require them to do community service right here at Garfield High School. Have them pick up trash, clean the walls, sweep the driveways, clean bathrooms and perform service projects on the Garfield campus. These players had taken the law into their own hands so let them learn now about consequences. It was time for them to be taught a real-life lesson.

The second measure, presented with just a few minutes remaining, was going to be more difficult to implement. Because of some very strong stances taken by the most outspoken of our female staff members, it was concluded that not only are we a society with rewards and punishments, but psychological interventions have an important role. We have psychologists who work with children who have problems, and these players clearly had problems.

"It's time," they declared, "to call in an expert. These football players need to be retrained."

Unfortunately, time was running out and there were a few teachers who had already lined up at the back door, wanting to leave. But they couldn't leave until that one last item was decided:

"Isn't it true," several teachers stated, "that psychologists routinely reprogram people, change their brain chemistry, and systematically adjust their mental circuitry? Isn't it true that this is what psychology and therapy are all about?"

As the school's psychologist and as a person who had taken many classes dealing with a variety of psychological issues and interventions, I had never heard therapy described in this manner. Someone asked: "Who should this psychologist be to reprogram and retrain these athletes?" And one of the more vocal female teachers responded with: "It should be a female therapist. We need a really good one so that these players can't escape from her expert psychological techniques."

With this last recommendation our time was up. I breathed a sigh of relief, happy that the meeting was over and that I could now get back to my standard duties. Teachers began leaving when one last question arose: "Who is going to find this female therapist?"

"Dick can do it," someone said and all the teachers' hands went up. The meeting was now over.

The following day I was informed by the principal that she had checked and rechecked the school's funds and had determined that the school could not afford to pay for some outside professional to come in and talk with these players. "Just don't have the money," she said. "Spent it on other things. See what you can find out there. Maybe this person would be willing to do it for free?"

Well, with no money, and with me having little interest or confidence in this process anyway, I decided to do what I considered to be the most appropriate response, nothing. About a week later, however, I received a phone call from Fran Cartmell, one of our English teachers: "Have you found a therapist?" she asked.

"No." I didn't want to tell her that I hadn't made even one inquiry.

"I've got someone who I think is good and her name is Starr Vega."

Fran gave me her phone number so I immediately called and, after talking with her, I knew that if anyone could accomplish what these teachers desired, she was the one. Ms. Vega was reasonable and not unrealistic about the task before her. She was aware of the difficulties she would be encountering. And not only was she willing to come in by herself, but she was willing to do it for free. I contacted the varsity football coach and gave him all the necessary information. The final responsibility for arranging this session was in his hands.

"She's great," I told him. "She and I had a good conversation on the phone and I explained what happened. I think she's competent and she's willing do if for free."

Unfortunately, four weeks later and with just two days before the end of the fall semester I received an emergency phone call from coach: "I couldn't get a hold of her. I've tried and tried, but she doesn't return my calls. Can you do the meeting with the players?"

I didn't respond and then I thought: *Oh my God. I meant to follow up with her, but I never did. I just got overwhelmed with work. Oh my God!*

"You're our last hope. And you have more experience with these kinds of things than anyone else. You run groups with the students and you moderated for the faculty. You do this type of thing all the time."

Coach and I were friends and we had talked many times. I'd even worked with some of his players individually and in my Focus groups.

"If you don't do it, no one will."

My stomach churned as I thought about what he was asking. But I was the school psychologist and a support person for the entire school. And I also knew that I had not followed through with another phone call to this person.

"Yes, I'll do it."

I had agreed to do this, but I wasn't comfortable with the proposed arrangement of me doing it alone with these fifty or so players. I believed a team approach was needed and I set about organizing such a team. I began with the head football coach and he agreed to participate. I talked with our school police officer and he agreed to be a part of the team approach. I discussed my idea with two of our stronger female teachers who would be able to present their side to the players, and I talked with the union representative. He, too, needed to be involved. All of these individuals were in agreement. But there was one last person who needed to part of this team approach, the principal, and I believed her presence to be vital.

I went to her office and knocked on the door. She was seated at her desk. As I explained what my plan was a frown came over her face. The faculty had wanted just one person reprogramming the football players, preferably a female psychologist, not a team. The coach had been unable to get a female therapist, but I was the next best thing. Her answer to this team approach was no. The next day, however, she recommended a female teacher who was considered to present a strong image on campus.

"Two people are better than one," I thought. I went to her classroom.

"I have no idea why the principal asked me to do this," she responded. "I was really surprised. The principal knows I don't think much of these football players. In fact I've had problems with several of them. The ones I've met are total asses." She paused, "But then I told the principal, 'Oh, what the hell, you only live once. I'll talk with these macho Mexican players."

We both laughed.

"Oh, what the hell," she said again, "they're all a bunch of male-macho teenagers who only think of themselves; but there are some things that I want to tell them."

"I, too, have just a few things I want to say. Let's make it short and get out of there."

We laughed again, and thus concluded our joint planning session. It was brief, but it covered what we considered to be the pertinent issues: the players were a bunch of male-macho adolescents and whatever it was that we intended to say, it shouldn't be much. Get in and get out.

The two of us recognized that these players had many difficulties and that the recommendations from the teachers' meeting were on the unrealistic side.

The meeting was scheduled for ten o'clock the following morning in the band room. I started for the door, but as I was about to exit, she yelled, "At ten o'clock tomorrow morning I'm giving my last final. I'll be there as just as soon as the office sends me a substitute."

CHAPTER 17

BULLDOG RUSH

PART THREE

The fall semester was almost over with only two periods remaining. Retraining was scheduled for the second period and when this class ended everyone would be dismissed to Christmas break. Each of the two periods would last for two hours and at twelve-thirty school officially ended.

I had done my preparation and written down a list of items I wanted to cover. And before this session began I had the additional opportunity to clarify my thoughts even more. I knew that this group of athletes could be very difficult. Coach, in fact, had informed me earlier that he had worked and worked with all of them throughout the season, but he felt he made little progress:

"I've had to throw more players off the team this year than in any of the past years, and they still don't change."

So as I thought about my strategy and what techniques I might employ, I had no great aspirations. In fact I had only one goal: get out of there as quickly as possible. But, and I felt quite good about this, I did have one reinforcement to aid in this process. There was the other female teacher who would be joining me. However, since I was the school psychologist it would be my responsibility to discuss some of the most crucial concerns expressed at the teachers' meeting. The other teacher would go first and then I would follow. We were scheduled to meet in the band room.

At ten o'clock and just after the morning break, approximately forty to fifty players wandered back and forth on the sidewalk leading to the band room. The two large metal doors remained closed and locked and I was the only adult present. The head coach should have been there but he had not yet arrived, and the assistant coaches were nowhere in sight. Not sure of what I should be doing, I climbed to the top of the stairs and watched the players. In many ways they appeared to be like a herd of restless cattle, agitated, upset, and keeping an eye out for what might be trouble. Suddenly all of their heads turned in my direction; in unison they all stared at me. Their eyes glared as they checked me out. What strategies might I employ to emasculate them? Psychologists, after all, do strange things. Would I be placing electrodes in their brains? Would I shrink their heads? Would I attempt to do something to their testicles? What scientific tactics had I learned to reprogram their deficient mental circuitry? I tried not to look uncomfortable as I stood there, but it was chilling. My eyes searched for the other coaches and they were not to be seen. My eyes scanned for that lone female teacher, but she, too, was missing.

Two or three of the players began pushing each other, hard pushes causing collisions into the walls of the adjacent classrooms where students were in class. "Thunk! Thud! Crash!" One player took up a challenging stance and looked me in the eye, keeping his hands at his sides. His back was slightly bent and his head down, but he kept staring. His fingers juxtaposed in various directions. "White fence," he mumbled. One hand had three or four fingers curled up and the other hand had three or four fingers curled down. His eyes glared as he again said, "White fence."

With his demonstration of inner-city life I finally understood. I was the enemy and I was being challenged like I was a rival of an opposing gang, or of an opposing football team. I was someone to be conquered. *White fence*, I repeated quietly in my mind along with, *What have I gotten myself in for?*

Another player moved around slowly between the others. He had a Kleenex box placed mysteriously over his right hand. The box had a Christmas wrapping on it, giving it the appearance of being a Christmas present. Then, and he did this while presenting the image of innocence, he would go up to an unsuspecting athlete and ask him to remove the wrapping and open the box. This person, upon removing the wrapping, suddenly and surprisingly found himself staring at the middle finger that was concealed inside the box. Raucous laughter accompanied the insult.

Pushing and shoving intensified with groups of players charging into each other...and then just as suddenly as it started it came to a halt. In mass they stopped and again stared. Anger showed upon their faces. While all of the other athletes were already on their way home, they had been left behind to endure this one last bit of punishment. They knew I was the reason they had not been permitted to leave on an early Christmas vacation dismissal.

"I don't need a psychologist," a player shouted. He yelled it again, even louder. "I don't need a psychologist. I'm not sick."

My mind kicked in to overdrive: *What am I doing here? How did I get myself into this mess? This is ridiculous. But I am the school psychologist and I've been asked by a friend to do this. I knew it wasn't going to be easy. We do what we can do to help others. What am I doing here?*

In front of me and to my sides the entire area exploded. More pushes and shoves, and players began ricocheting in every direction, when finally down the cement path and walking quite rapidly came the head coach. He was wearing his characteristic baseball cap and blue shorts. He climbed the stairs where I had taken refuge and spoke to all of us: "We're not meeting in this room. We're moving over to MH-2."

The band room, which had been the initial selection for this meeting, was the better choice of the two rooms. The band room was large, somewhat new, and it had cushioned seating in a terraced arrangement. There were no movable chairs or tables, and in this room it would have been relatively easy to confine these players within these seats. MH-2 (Math Hall-2) on the other hand, was a poor choice. It was old and dingy, and its primary purpose was for the Mariachi band. MH-2 was the practice room. A raised wooden floor served as a kind of stage and it was placed in the front. Everything was movable, and overall it presented the appearance of disarray as well as a lack of control and organization.

Coach led us to our newly assigned room, but you could hear the grumblings: "Why are we meeting in this room? The other room is better." I, too, had the same concerns, but the room selection was not our decision.

We followed coach, who was about five feet eight and weighed in at around a hundred and sixty pounds. He was tiny but very compact and, at times, he had a reputation of being a loose cannon. He was Mighty Mouse with an attitude. Years earlier he had bench pressed three hundred pounds, almost twice his body weight. Coach's muscles rippled through his knit shirt and over the past years he had proven himself to be one of the most successful football coaches in the Los Angeles Unified School District. Each year our team was one of the district's most successful. When we reached the new location, he pulled out a key and opened the door.

I was the first to go in, hoping that by doing so I would have a clearer idea of how I should handle myself in this unexpected environment. I went to the front section and stood on the makeshift wooden floor and I knew... I was in trouble. I could see that this project and my idea of getting out of there as quickly as possible might prove to be a little more difficult than anticipated. No, it was going to be a lot more difficult.

There was a tall stool placed in the front and I sat on it. I watched each player, slowly and with expressions of dissatisfaction, find his desired location, his own personal territory to call his own. It was an arduous and slow process as they aligned themselves. Just like on the football field, they were picking their spots and getting a feel for the surroundings and the opposing team. Some sat with their desks turned backwards. Others clumped several chairs together, constructing a kind of barricade.

I watched and felt faint. The more a person builds these kinds of barricades around himself, the more likely there is some type of emotional maladjustment. I'd seen this before when I was working in a school for students with severe emotional problems. The principal had asked me to run a group and it was an experience I would never forget. They all built barricades around themselves, challenging everyone and everything from their perceived protection. This group never progressed and after several weeks I cancelled it. The football players were doing the same thing.

My stomach churned as I watched more barricades being constructed. I leaned forward on my metal stool trying to catch my breath and to make some sort of a plan to handle whatever might happen. And it was at that moment I realized what I should have known all along. These players had a full five weeks to mentally prepare themselves for this final showdown. Psychological services, therapy, group discussion, all require that the person or persons involved be receptive and open to these services. These players weren't open or receptive. A shiver went up and down my spine. This was war and I could see that they were digging in. They had prepared themselves well for what they knew was my goal, brainwash them and reprogram their circuits.

I remained on the metal stool with my legs clasping the sides. These players were ready for any tricks, if I had any, but I did not. I placed the few materials that I had brought with me, several pages of loosely scribbled notes on the wooden platform to the side of the metal stool. Six or seven of the more resistant players stood on the sidelines, remaining by the door and the exit, not wanting to come in or sit down.

"There are a few more seats," I called out. I motioned with my hands. "I want everyone to find a place."

No one moved.

"I want everyone to sit down!"

We were ready to begin and at this point there were three coaches standing on the side: the head coach and two assistant coaches. They stood far to the rear and by the open door. The head coach closed the door. Everyone was now present and it was time to get started, but we sat. The players looked at me, and I turned to the head football coach. For these first few moments, it appeared that no one had any idea about what we were doing or why we had even decided to come into this room. And maybe, just maybe, that was the truth of the situation? The coaches remained to the side and I sat on my metal stool. Nothing happened.

Finally, when it was apparent that someone had to step to the front and get this last piece of punishment started, one of the assistant coaches came forward. He stood about three yards to my left. At last the time had arrived to begin. This assistant coach looked out to the team, but on his face was not the expression of a coach of one of the finest teams in the city. On his face was a look of disappointment, a look shared by the entire coaching staff.

This coach began: "Today is your last day of atonement. You are to hear from the school psychologist and learn why you act as you do."

His words rang in my ears: "Your last day of atonement. You are to learn why you act as you do."

I almost fell off the tall metal stool. *This assistant coach had almost two months to think about what he was going to say and this was the best that he could come up with?*

The coach continued: "He's going to talk with you and then the season is done. This is it. This is the last thing that you have to go through. After this your punishment is over."

He returned to the security of the corner and the head coach replaced him.

Coach walked slowly to the front, keeping his head down. The baseball cap, which was one of coach's trademarks, remained on his head. There was complete silence. Coach stood with his head down, and then it rose. More silence. This was possibly going to be the last time coach would address these players as a full team. What was he going to say? This team had beaten almost every team in the city. His eyes scanned the team, from one side of the room to the other; it was a true mishmash of people. Players clumped chairs around themselves. Some sat together, while others remained separated from their peers. These separated players were the isolates, the individuals who got along with no one and there were many of these.

Coach's eyes looked at each one of them, and he knew them all, inside and out. His head went down. After about twenty seconds, he looked up and tears had formed in his eyes. He tried not to show any emotion, but that was not possible: "I've had to throw more players off the team this year than in any year in the past, and still your attitudes are bad."

Silence.

"Right now we are not going to have a football banquet. The seniors on this team have not taken the leadership that is necessary. If we are to have a banquet, there are people that need to be invited and it is the seniors who are responsible for this."

Coach stopped. His eyes again scanned from the left to the right, and then to the front. Even as these players sat listening to their coach, they had the look of an unruly mob.

"It looks to me like there will be no banquet and that is really too bad. As a team you have done some things that no one else has done. There are only three other schools in the city that have done what you have accomplished. You have gone to the 4A City Championships four years in a row. Only Banning, Carson and San Fernando have accomplished this. If the seniors don't get this organized, there will be no banquet."

He had said his piece and it was time to get this final chastisement over with: "Mr. Selby is here to talk with you. Listen to what he has to say," and he walked out the door. The other coaches went with him.

It was almost fifty of these varsity players and the one of me. There were more maneuverings, with a few scrapes and nudges of tables, but then they were ready. The shrink had arrived and just let him try to pull a fast one. Just let him try to shrink their heads. In fact it didn't matter what this psychologist had to say. They had come to this meeting begrudgingly, but now that they were here it was going to be real payback. I picked up my notes and turned my eyes to the front and began: "I'm here because of what happened."

At last I was underway and as I began I even surprised myself. I presented the appearance of calmness and determination. I maintained good eye contact and to all of the players it seemed as though I knew what I was doing.

"I'm here because the teachers requested that someone such as myself talk with the team. They were very upset over what had happened."

The players listened and did not respond. In fact the entire room was surprisingly quiet. They sat and watched with all of their eyes focused on me. Who was I? They didn't know what to expect from some kind of psychologist but they all knew… I was trained in my profession and my specialty was thumping narcissistic and unruly football players. They knew why I was there. They also were aware, as I was about to learn, that one teacher had called for "their balls to be cut off." As a result of everything that had happened, they had come to the unanimous understanding that all of the teachers in the school hated them.

They waited patiently, perhaps out of a concern to hear what I was going to say, and perhaps out of some vague concern for self-improvement. But mostly they were quiet because of the possibility that the coaches might make an unexpected and impromptu return. They had to give this psychologist thing some time to evolve, in order to make sure no one was going to quickly open the door and rush in.

I continued: "Because of Bulldog Rush three meetings were held with the teachers. At all of these meetings the teachers were extremely upset over what had happened and they felt that it was necessary for some actions to be taken."

Five minutes had past and the coaches had not made an unscheduled return. All was safe. From the corner: "The teachers don't care about us. They put us down. They think our balls should be cut off."

From the other side: "They just think football players are nothing. All they do is try to get us into trouble."

There was no longer any reason to fake it. They were mad and as a result of the three teacher meetings they had been treated like common criminals. They had been treated like the men who pick up papers along the freeways. Why would they have to do this? They weren't getting the respect they deserved. After all, as a team they had the best record of any of the school's previous football teams, and they had been required to perform campus clean up. Someone was going to be retrained all right, but it wasn't going to be them. Voices sprang from every location and many had shifted from sitting on their chairs to standing on them. It was fifty against one.

Sometime later, and I'm not sure how long it took, they sat down and I continued: "The teachers were upset. They were upset with the football team and they were upset with the head coach. This was very serious. Because of what happened he could have lost his job."

From the left corner: "Get rid of coach." And from the other side: "Who cares about him. He's nothing." There came another explosion only louder than before. Players stood on their chairs. Some pointed fingers while others shouted. *What had I gotten myself in for?* My legs squeezed tightly to the iron rails of my metal stool. In this bedlam my metal stool had become my security blanket.

I watched and felt faint. Coaches set a model for students and the interactions between the coach and his players are what guide many a young man. The high school coach, whether it's in football or any of the other sports, is frequently the most revered man in a young student's life. These players didn't respect coach and they were openly defiant and derogatory.

"When it's quiet," I stated, and my voice surprisingly appeared to be in command, "we can get started again."

Now, before progressing any further with what was happening, it is necessary to explain what was really going on. These players didn't want to change. They were happy being the way they were... and even if they weren't happy, they weren't going to admit that to anyone. These were macho-adolescent males with exploding levels of testosterone, striving to prove their virility with every passing minute. Unhappiness, dissatisfaction with previous actions or feelings, putting women or teachers down, these were all issues that were actively being avoided by most of them. And what does sensitivity and caring about others have to do with proving who is the most macho? They were winning football games and that was what life was about, not helping people or being recognized as being kind or compassionate

So there we were, one school psychologist foolishly trapped by his own short sightedness and lack of understanding of the situation, and the fifty of them. What was I going to do? What could I do?

When their initial tactics of standing and pointing fingers didn't bring the desired result, which was to bring me to my knees and publicly make me submit (walk out, cry, blow up), in unison they began laughing. Yes, I knew that what I was attempting was insanity.

Why didn't I just get up and leave? This was what they wanted and maybe this is what I should have done, but I didn't. I had committed myself to this project and, unfortunately, there are times in life when it's difficult to change in mid-stream. So what did I do? Well, I did nothing. I sat there and simply did not react. I sat calmly and waited, and as I sat there something interesting happened. The room quieted down.

When it had quieted, I said: "While I'm here I'm not going to put anyone down. We're just going to talk."

More laughter and again players stood on their chairs. Payback wasn't going to elude them. After all, they had waited weeks for this opportunity. But as I sat in front of these fifty varsity champions I had an idea. I realized their task was to break me down, to make me suffer and to make me succumb to their dominance. As I looked out to them I realized I had to make a choice: to play this game out, or to head for the hills. They were laughing and taunting, and in this atmosphere of chaos and raucous laughter I had to do something to get control. Then, and without showing even the slightest emotion or upset, I said, "I feel like I should be a comedian."

My eyes squared with theirs. Could they believe what I had just said? Could I believe what I had just said? More laughter and several pounded their hands upon the desks. They pointed. There were a few who even thumped their chests. In their world of football, the inner city, and of being macho adolescents, laughing and taunting are considered to be surest way to make someone angry, the surest way to breakdown a perceived opponent. They jumped. They thumped. They hollered and laughed, but I was still right there in front of them. My eyes remained straightforward. I was calm, undisturbed, and outwardly not even the slightest upset by their tactics.

"I feel like I should go on the comedy channel."

What was I saying? Didn't I know that I was supposed to be outraged? Didn't I know that I was supposed to call them names or walk out in disgust? They had tried anger, shouting, yelling, laughter, taunting, but no matter what they did I was still there, and I had not even reacted. Suddenly it become very clear that I wasn't just going to go away and that this thumping of the school psychologist was going to be a touch more difficult that they had at originally thought.

They looked at each other. Those who had been standing on their chairs and pounding their chests began to sit down. The room quieted and the atmosphere changed. Everyone took his seat. What were they going to do now? No, they weren't done, but it was time to regroup. Time to rethink their strategy.

This successful handling of the disturbance marked the end of the first quarter. In my mind they were still ahead, but as least I had been able to turn it into a contest. I looked down at my notes and in front of me were the issues I wanted to discuss, but I was not yet ready to begin. Control is the name of the game in football and control is the name of the game for the reprogramming of varsity football players. There were a few last attempts with laughter and my eye squared with these individuals.

"You guys are really making me feel good. You're getting me ready for the comedy channel." The room was quiet.

The stage was now set for me to begin: "I've been asked to speak to you because the teachers have some concerns. I have written these down and I will read them. I am not going to put anyone on the spot but I would like to hear what you think of them." I tried to speak slowly and clearly. "One of the primary things was that some of the teachers felt that we should no longer have football here."

"Get rid of football," from one person in the rear.

"Who cares about it?" came from another.

And from another: "I'm a senior. Who cares what they do?"

These answers didn't just reflect their attitudes, but these were the same reactions that caused them to be in this predicament in the first place. The only thing that was going to change these players was life itself: life, with its good times and its bad. In thirty, forty, or fifty years most of them would modify their behaviors. Some, however, would be resistant to any kind of modification and self-introspection, and a few would likely find themselves in prison.

So what was my goal? It had not changed. My plan was to get in and get out as soon as possible. These players were waiting for any opening to attack. I proceeded with my list of concerns:

1. The football players are a bunch of male chauvinists.
2. They continually put women down.
3. They do not respect the opposite sex.
4. They use bad language and frequently make derogatory sexual comments.
5. They are a mob.
6. They expect preferential treatment because they are on the football team.

For about half-an-hour, and this was to my surprise and my relief, some sort of a discussion took place, though the elements of this discussion were not what you would call earth-shattering, endearing, or representative on any type of emotional growth. According to them, the teachers were to blame. The administration didn't understand them. The counselors didn't give them special privileges, like writing them free passes when they were tardy or letting them cut in the lunch lines whenever they wanted. It was clear in their way of thinking that no one understood them, and after one-half hour it all came down to this: the reason why they had rioted and acted as they did was everyone else's fault.

I followed my notes and as I progressed I kept my eyes fixed on the last one. When I was able to reach that most important final one, dealing with the idea that because they were on the football team they should be allotted special treatment, all of the teachers list of important concerns had been discussed. Were these players now reprogrammed? If they were, I certainly had nothing to do with it. What about the brain chemistry and mental circuits? Had these been altered in any way? Not that I was aware of, but one most important fact did stand out and to me it was significant. I had survived, and that was my goal. So what if it was my brain that was the one being reprogrammed. But I had learned first hand from this experience that this entire idea was ridiculous and I would never be involved with anything like this again.

"It's time to go," I said and I motioned to the door for them to leave. They all sat, not wanting to go. They were unable to define what had happened as a victory for their side and they weren't about to call it quits. Hands sprang up: "We want to talk some more. We want to make it clear how bad these teachers are. We want you to help us cut in front of the lunch lines."

Resistance, in and of itself, can be a sign of emotional maladjustment. The more resistant someone is, the more can be the anger, the hostility and the maladjustment. These players were very resistant.

"The teachers just put us down. No one cares about us. It's all everyone else's fault."

But at this point whatever they wanted to say or had hoped to say, it was too late. Each player had been provided ample opportunity to state his opinion and I was done. Discussion was over. Most of the players rose from their seats and started for the door, but, unfortunately, the other teacher arrived. She had been unable to leave her class. "Couldn't get a sub," she said. "And then when the sub came I didn't know what room to go to. Am I too late?"

The players looked at her. Here was someone who had suddenly been added to the playing field, and maybe, just maybe, this game wasn't over after all. There might be an over time. One player shouted: "Teachers at this school just try to put us down. No one listens."

She looked at him and was completely surprised, but she did not respond. Then someone at the back stood on his chair and yelled: "Teachers don't care about us. All they care about is themselves. All teachers want to do is punk us." Again she did not respond.

Quietly I informed her that the retraining project was completed and that the players were leaving. "It's time to go," I reaffirmed, and I repeated it. Slowly they rose from their spots, those safe havens that had become so precious to them, and made their way to the door. There were various comments, of which I paid no attention, but making sure that all of them left.

After the last person had gone through the door and we exited, she asked: "How did it go?"

"Let me think about this for awhile. I'm not really sure." I closed the door and at last it was over.

Bulldog Rush and the behavior of the football players continued to be a point of contention for many of the teachers. As it turned out, the person who arranged for this unsanctioned activity was an aide who worked at the school. In the future he would find himself in even more trouble and as a result he would be dismissed both from his job and from the school.

The concerns and the many complaints about Bulldog rush continued to reverberate throughout Garfield for the remainder of this school year. The coach, even though he had a winning record, eventually transferred to a different position. And at the conclusion of this school year and partially because of this incident, even though it had occurred without her consent or awareness, the principal was transferred.

Bulldog Rush was never held again.

CHAPTER 18

EDUCATORS MAKING A DIFFERENCE

This book began with a dedication to John Benson. John Benson was a teacher, a dean, and a coach of several sports. He worked at Garfield for thirty-nine years, retiring in 2004. In the years since his retirement, John has dedicated himself to an ongoing scholarship program that provides scholarships to Garfield's graduating seniors. It is called the John Benson Scholarship Program and in 2012 it provided approximately forty-two thousand dollars to Garfield's seniors. John has not done this all by himself but has worked with a committee comprised entirely of Garfield alumni. They are Linda Contreras Cuadra, Carlos Venegas, Frances Salazar, and Ralph Moran. These are the original alumni that started the program. The following alumni have also helped in this process: Jema Estrella, Raquel Garcia, Javier Gonzalez, Jeanice Hori, Irma Jauregui, Carmen Martinez, Brian Moon, Jose Resado, Larry Romero, Thelma Romero, Robert Trujillo, and Faviola Vega.

John Benson stands out as being exceptional in his dedication to Garfield and its students, but there were many others who also provided exemplary service.

Harold Manyweather was in charge of both the music department and the marching band. Almost every year his marching bands proved to be the finest in the entire Los Angeles Unified School District. While most schools had twenty or thirty musicians in their marching bands, Garfield frequently fielded more than sixty musicians. Harold Manyweather was a soft-spoken teacher and band leader who everyone admired. Victory trophies filled the walls of the band room.

Jacqui Heiland worked at Garfield for forty-nine years. She began there in 1956 and retired in 2005. Jacqui was an advocate of empowering Garfield students. She took a variety of leadership roles and was a strong believer of counseling and support services. Jacqui provided a positive influence at Garfield High School for almost fifty years.

Lee Patterson was in charge of the Drop-out-Prevention Program. Her expertise and her compassionate nature helped students to remain in school when they were experiencing problems. She frequently could be seen intervening on their behalf, sometimes with the deans and at other times with the counselors. Lee was responsible for initiating the counseling program with the school psychologist that provided counseling services to many thousands of students.

Greta Gutierrez taught in the ESL department. She was actively involved in maintaining quality programs that would benefit the entire school. Greta was a natural leader, having a positive effect on everyone with whom she worked.

Alberto Palacios served as a teacher, as the coordinator of the ESL Department, and as the union representative. Because of his many responsibilities he frequently found himself in a position that placed him in conflict with the various principals. Alberto was a strong leader who remained focused on meeting the needs of the school and the teachers whom he represented. Alberto was always willing to take the necessary steps to help the school move forward. Even though Alberto has retired, he continues to be active both at Garfield and within the community of East Los Angeles. Currently he is involved in the political arena, aligning himself with the movement to have East Los Angeles become separate from Los Angeles and become its own incorporated city.

Three other teachers will be mentioned together: Tom Woessner, Lucy Romero and John Bennett. These three joined forces working with Garfield's Academic Decathlon Team. Year after year they spent many hundreds of hours preparing Garfield students for the difficult competitions. It was because of their united efforts that these Garfield students demonstrated a high degree of success in the citywide competitions. Each of these individuals was also an excellent teacher, bringing their knowledge and their love for the students into the classroom.

And last but not least is Jose Huerta. Jose was a teacher, a dean, and an assistant principal at Garfield. Due to Jose's many competencies he has worked himself up the administrative ladder. He is currently Garfield's principal. Under his guidance, with the cooperation of the teachers and the students, Garfield has become one of the most successful schools in the inner city for raising student academic levels. Jose has not done this single-handedly, but his positive attitude and professionalism has helped lead Garfield to the forefront on what can be achieved within the inner city school and at a minority school.

There were many other teachers, counselors and support personnel that also worked far beyond what was required of them. I regret that I cannot share all of their names, but their love of the students and their love of teaching helped the school to function successfully.

Yes, Garfield High School is in East Los Angeles and the students have similar disadvantages to students in other inner city schools:

poverty, gangs, drugs, limited English proficiency. However, it is also a school with a tradition of representing something special to its student body. Jaime Escalante, the famous math teacher, exemplified the kind of success that can be achieved through hard work and a love of the students. Jaime gave Garfield an important start, but in many respects Garfield's overall success is just now beginning. Academic achievement levels have risen consistently over the years. Thirteen years ago the API scores were in the low five hundreds. In 2011, the API index has improved to 707, placing it at the forefront of similar inner city schools. The future of Garfield remains bright and with the leadership that it now has, as well as its quality staff, more success is on the way.

This book comes to a close and the stories within it reflect upon a different time and a different generation from that of today. Yes, there were some difficult situations and events, but that is to be expected whenever one goes into education. Though I am no longer at Garfield the memories remain. I consider myself fortunate to have experienced all that I did, both the good and the bad, during my sixteen years at the school. And I know that as I look back on all of these experiences I will state with fondness that "I am and will forever be a Garfield Bulldog."

ABOUT THE AUTHOR

Dick Selby graduated from UCLA with a degree in psychology in 1968. While he was at UCLA he was on the school's track team. He became the school record holder in the javelin and was honored as an "All-American" athlete in track and field. He was also a member of the 1966 UCLA "NCAA Championship Track and Field Team." That 1966 track team is considered to be one of the most dominant track teams in the history of the NCAA.

In 1970, Dick began working for the Los Angeles Unified School District where he remained for thirty-four years. He worked as a school psychologist for approximately twenty-four years. Twice he was selected as a "School Psychologist of the Year," and in the year 2000, he was honored by Channel 13 (KCOP) as their "Hero of the Week."

Dick earned a Master's Degree in Counseling from what is now known as The Phillips Graduate Institute. He earned his Pupil Personnel Services Credential in School Psychology from the University of Pepperdine. He is both a Licensed Marriage and Family Therapist and a Licensed Educational Psychologist.

Along with Dick's academic success, he has also made thirteen trips to India, traveling to the ashram of Sai Baba. Sai Baba is believed by many to be one of the most important spiritual influences India has seen in the last one hundred years. Dick has written three books about these experiences with Sai Baba, all of which are published in India. Dick has written two books that are published in the United States: *A School Psychologist in East L.A*, and *1963, Oceanside High School.*